LEGAL

CW00498799

Section 6 Criminal Law Act 1977
As Amended by Criminal Justice and Public Order Act 1994

TAKE NOTICE

THAT we live in this property, it is our home and we intend to stay here.

THAT at all times there is at least one person in this property.

THAT any entry or attempt to enter into this property without our permission is a criminal offence as any one of us who is in physical possession is opposed to entry without our permission.

THAT if you attempt to enter by violence or by threatening violence we will prosecute you. You may receive a sentence of up to six months imprisonment and/or a fine of up to £5,000.

THAT if you want to get us out you will have to take out a summons for possession in the County Court or in the High Court, or to produce to us a written statement or certificate in terms of S.12 A Criminal Law Act, 1977 (as inserted by Criminal Justice and Public Order Act, 1994).

THAT it is an offence under S.12 A (8) Criminal Law Act 1977 (as amended) to knowingly make a false statement to obtain a written statement for the purposes of S.12 A. A person guilty of such an offence may receive a sentence of up to six months imprisonment and/or a fine of up to £5,000.

Signed

The Occupiers

N.B. **Signing this Legal Warning is optional. It is equally valid whether or not it is signed.**

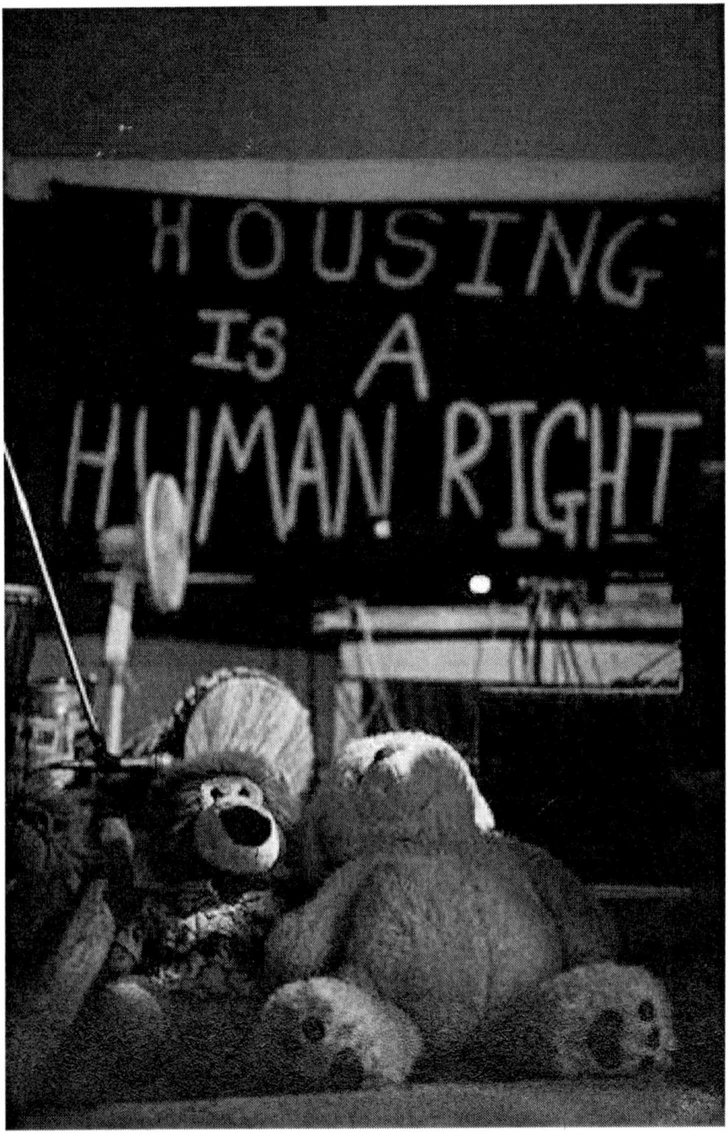
HOUSING
IS A
HUMAN RIGHT

Total Shambles

George F.

Influx Press, London

Published by Influx Press
Office 3A, Mill Co. Project,
Unit 3, Gaunson House
Markfield Road, London, N15 4QQ
www.influxpress.com

First published 2015

Printed and bound in the UK by the Short Run Press Ltd., Exeter

ISBN 978-1910312049

To all the crews, past present and new.
And Mum and Dad too.

Contents

Disclaimer:

Although the contents of this book are based on the actual experiences of George F. whilst squatting in London, certain literary licence has been taken with the names of people, dates and locations that have been changed in order to protect both the innocent and the guilty.

This work should be read as a piece of creative non-fiction.

Total Shambles

George F.

total (tōt′al)

adj.

1. Of, relating to, or constituting the whole; entire.
2. Complete; utter; absolute: *total concentration; a total effort; a total fool.*

shambles (shâm′balz)

pl.n. (used with a sing. verb)

1.
a. A scene or condition of complete disorder or ruin:
'*The economy was in a shambles*' (W. Bruce Lincoln).
b. Great clutter or jumble; a total mess:
made dinner and left the kitchen a shambles.

2.
a. A place or scene of bloodshed or carnage.
b. A scene or condition of great devastation.

3. A slaughterhouse.

4. *Archaic*: A meat market or butcher shop.

[From Middle English shamel, shambil, place where meat is butchered and sold, from Old English sceamol, table, from Latin scabillum, scamillum, diminutive of scamnum, bench, stool.]

Word History:

A place or situation referred to as a *shambles* is usually a mess, but it is no longer always the bloody mess it once was. The history of the word begins innocently enough with the Latin word *scamnum*, 'a stool or bench serving as a seat, step, or support for the feet, for example.' The diminutive *scamillum*, 'low stool,' was borrowed by speakers of Old English as *sceamol*, 'stool, bench, table.' Old English *sceamol* became Middle English *shamel*, which developed the specific sense in the singular and plural of 'a place where meat is butchered and sold.' The Middle English compound *shamelhouse* meant 'slaughterhouse,' a sense that the plural *shambles* developed (first recorded in 1548) along with the figurative sense 'a place or scene of bloodshed' (first recorded in 1593). Our current, more generalized meaning, 'a scene or condition of disorder,' is first recorded in 1926.

Definitions taken from: http://www.thefreedictionary.com

A Pot Head History of Squatting

Squatting is the oldest mode of tenure in the world, and we are all descended from squatters. This is as true of the Queen with her 176,000 acres as it is of . . . householders in Britain who are owner-occupiers. They are all the ultimate recipients of stolen land, for to regard our planet as a commodity offends every conceivable principle of natural rights.

— Colin Ward

To squat is to reject one of the core principles of the social contract we are born into and bound by — that of the sanctity of property ownership. To fully comprehend the significance of squatting requires an understanding of its place in history, as the cutting edge of a tradition dating back centuries to a time before the concept of owning property, of land ownership, even existed. Squatting was first defined by those who were not squatters. Those with power can deprive others of the materials necessitous to survival, of the means of supporting themselves, and thus make those with less power dependent on the strong for survival. In Britain, this arguably began with the Romans seizing land and power from the Celts, who arguably deprived the native Britons of it. The Romans were the first State in Britain, however, and the first imperialists. The Latin model of land-ownership, as well as the legislature and centralisation of power was continued by the Normans, who imposed a system of land control and domination on the ragtag mongrel nations of bearded marauder-gangs monikered Vikings, Danes, Jutes and Angles who had sailed over and squatted Great Britain after some unpleasant pillaging, as well as specialising in designing a system of power that was linguistic as well as physical. This model is still actively engaged in alienating the commoners, through its evolution as the jargon of law known as *legalese*.

The massive depopulation of England during the Black Death (roughly 50% of the population succumbed in Britain) lead not only to an abundance of vacant land (and indeed entire villages) but also to a skyrocketing of the value of labour. Due to a dearth of available workers, labourers could wrangle a fair wage from the lords. Those uppity peasants even began to buy luxury goods once reserved exclusively for the aristocrats, resulting in the legislating of unsuccessful enforced consumption laws to prohibit such effrontery. Beginning to wonder why they needed someone lording it over them since they were doing all the work and reaping little of the reward, peasants began to organise to end serfdom, setting up their own communities which were independent of the manor system in place at that time. The lords and ladies responded by repeatedly trying to impose poll taxes upon the people and to criminalise such autonomous actions — a tactic of blunt extortion not to be repeated until the 1990s by Margaret Thatcher's government, and with similar results. In 1990, we had the Poll Tax riots — nearly 600 years earlier, attempts by aristocracy to bureaucratically mug the people resulted in the Peasant's Revolt. When its most famous leader, Wat Tyler, was murdered and betrayed at Blackheath, the subsequent nationwide rebellions were mercilessly crushed. Property rights became sacrosanct.

If you so much as strolled through a festival or owned a radio in the 90s, you will have heard of the Diggers, though perhaps by the name made popular by crusty-festival favourites of the dreadlock-and-cider crew, the True Levellers. If you have no idea what I'm talking about then go find a copy of *Levelling the Land* before reading on (and get a dog on a string while you're at it). In the 1600s, they were the epitome of the idealistic squatter, attempting to collectively farm common land, in the spirit of levelling real property, and invited all to join them in this spirit and share their ale and grain. As head Digger Gerard Winstanley stated: 'England is not a free people, till the poor that have no land, have a free allowance to dig and labour the commons and so live as comfortably as the landlords that live in their enclosures'. Much like their 20th century counterparts, they wanted to pull down all enclosures, share everything and have a bloody good time doing it. In a narrative that should be familiar to all *Evening Standard* readers, the Diggers were vilified, violently harassed, repeatedly evicted, accused of sexual perversion and subsequently denied the opportunity to defend themselves.

The Diggers were reacting against a piece of legislation called the Enclosures Act. The first one was passed in 1604, the last in 1911, with over 5,200 of them happening in the 300 years in between, succeeding in fencing off 6.8 million acres of public land. Prior to this, most land was termed 'common' or 'waste'. Common land was collectively owned, and normally subdivided between a number of peasants, workers and the local lord. 'Wasteland' was intrinsically available for the use of anyone without land to cultivate and do with however they saw best — which was normally growing food, grazing cattle or, outrageously, living on it. The trend in Enclosures Acts was sporadic up until the Industrial Revolution, when it was decided they didn't even need to go before Parliament anymore, where upon it became a tactic to drive the necessary workers (and indeed an excess of them) into the cities to slave in the factories or rot in the work-houses.

Packed into grimy, filthy, polluted, violent urban sprawl for a century, the workers of England suffered further during the Blitz of the Second World War. Hundreds of thousands of homes were destroyed, and thousands more left empty. Similar to when the Great Fire decimated vast parts of London in the 1600s, the opportunity was taken for a great social reorganisation by both employers and workers. In the spirit of self-determination, returning soldiers occupied empty buildings and military camps and began the process of rebuilding gutted neighbourhoods through direct action. Some of these camps existed until the 1950s. Returning soldiers occupied land and property across England en masse. Calling themselves the Vigilantes, within a year of the war's end there were nearly 40,000 ex-servicemen and their families squatting across the country. In *Cotters and Squatters: The Hidden History Of Housing*, by Colin Ward, it is described how Aneurin Bevan — people's champion of the NHS — ordered the gas and electricity cut to these camps, but by that time local councils had already begun directing homeless people to some 1000 camps in order to house themselves. The camps featured communal cooking, work rotas and nursery services entirely self-organised by the occupiers.

In 1946, 1,500 people squatted mansion-houses in Pimlico, St. John's Wood and Kensington in an action called 'the Great Sunday Squat'. Five of the organisers of these incursions were arrested for 'conspiracy to incite trespass', though later released on good behaviour. The occupations were widely supported by Londoners who tried to deliver food to the besieged squatters by throwing it up at the windows like bread-grenades. Although being one of the biggest acts of civil disobedience in England's history, this popular revolt is largely absent from our cultural narrative. These Vigilantes represent that other branch of 'selfhousers' — namely, the pragmatic — who squat and challenge property laws not out of idealism, but out of necessity.

In the decades following the Second World War, the urban industrial centres declined. More people and businesses fled into the suburbs and countryside, in a reverse form of urbanisation that left vast swathes of England's major cities empty. Into these spaces, the dispossessed and self-determined moved in, creating entire streets of squatted buildings such as the Villa Road community in Brixton, and the Talacre estate in Kentish Town. Some of these existed for more than 30 years, before being overwhelmed by creeping gentrification. The might of squatters was fearsome, with a Squatter's Union formed to organise defence against bailiffs, complete with membership cards.

During the 1960s, the Family Squatting Movement forced councils across London to sign agreements with them in a coup now hailed as the beginning of the housing co-op movement in Britain. The making of agreements with councils was not greeted with enthusiasm by all the squatting communities, and before the ink was even dry on the contract, many members of the Family Squatting Movement broke away and formed what was to become the Advisory Service for Squatters.

Through the 1980s and 90s, the squatting movement in London terrorised local councils and fought back bitterly against bureaucratic incompetence and dismissal. In 1987, Hackney Town Hall was occupied repeatedly and monthly council meetings disrupted by squatters demanding an end to evictions whilst 3000 council houses remained empty. In 1988, 120 flats were squatted on the Stamford Hill estate and subsequently evicted by armies of riot police fighting over burning barricades. In 1994, over 30,000 people attended the Hackney Homeless Festival, despite encroachments and harassment by police under the new Criminal Justice Bill.

Since the turn of the Millennium, this defiance and idealism has continued to flourish across the UK, be it in the form of the Stoke's Croft riot in Bristol, against a proposed new Tesco store on their street, or the five year existence of a social centre on Rampart Street in Whitechapel up until 2009. Cardiff had the Gremlins in their disused bowling alley, Leeds the Commonplace, Nottingham the JB Spray building. Brighton became, and continues to be, a hub of activity against anti-squatting svengali Mike Weatherley MP, based around long-running activist hub the Cowley Club. The third runway has been confounded and delayed by the good folks living in caravans and tree houses at Grow Heathrow, despite the ongoing threat of eviction. In 2011, the Occupy movement seized the grounds outside St. Paul's and, in response to huge demand from participants, nearby Finsbury Square. For a season of self-organisation, public meetings featuring a cast of hundreds of idealistic activists, earnest students, middle-class sympathisers with babies slung on their backs and a militia of Special Brew chugging hardcore homeless were held for consensus decision making by a sea of waving hands (the activist group signal for agreement). For perhaps the first time, thousands of people were exposed and invited to the idea that they might have a direct and decisive voice in making choices that effected many more than just themselves. All through the months-long occupation, very central to its existence was a stringent disregard for zoning and planning permission. Occupy London was part of a global movement, yet only in the UK were participants able to open and actualise empty properties such as the Earl's Street Community Centre, the 'Hobo Hilton', and the Bank of Ideas (owned by the Royal Bank of Scotland), which saw performances and celebrity endorsements from Massive Attack and Thom Yorke of Radiohead. Despite the intimate and obvious connections, few commentators have made explicit links between the Occupy movement and squatting. Broadly speaking, both movements decried the inherent injustice and disparity of wealth and opportunity in our modern society. For a while, Occupy was a media-darling, yet when the police moved in en masse to tear down tents and harry gangs of newly homeless people around the City, the cameras seemed to have lost interest in that all important climax of the narrative.

The delineation between squatter and tenant isn't only a dispute between owner and occupier — as we have seen, the rejection of creative methods of self-housing comes from a higher source. Across London today, there are thousands of 'hidden homes' in commercial properties. Converted warehouses, storerooms above garages, even old toilet blocks have been secretly refurbished and occupied with the full knowledge and assistance of the owner who charges rents to people living there. These have recently come to the attention of the authorities, who are using planning legislation rather than trespass laws in order to clamp down on people's defiance of the law. People simply cannot be allowed to solve their own problems if their solutions fall outside the mandate of authority.

Criminalisation by the State has not been limited to the persecution of urban squatters, or as they were called by another, more neutral, name, 'self-housers'. Colin Ward also discusses how, up until 1939, plotlanders were a common and inspiring example of self-determination and self-help across the UK. Plotlands were small areas of land divided up by owners and sold on for development by owner-occupiers. Improved over generations, the plotlands served as holiday homes, retirement spaces, and sources of great personal pride for their owners. Squeezed on to grassy verges, next to railway lines, or on disused agricultural land, the plotlands were the property-owning democracy manifest, and were often self-built by owners over many years with little capital and no assistance from local councils. Often owned by renters from the city, they provided extra income as they hired them out to other holidaymakers, despite the lack of sewer systems and water only available from standpipes. The plotland developments were eventually wiped out by that tyrannical form of bureaucracy known as 'planner's blight'. Despite their ingenuity and dedication to self-improvement, the plotland developments were outside of authority's blessing, and therefore subject to the threat of the bulldozer.

Similarly stigmatised and persecuted by despotic planning regulations, travelling communities have also been targeted by a central government fanatical about quashing any autonomy from its populace. In 1994, the Criminal Justice Act made it an offence to park a caravan on land you did not own without permission, effectively criminalising the activities of travellers both New Age and traditional, and driving them into a life of endless eviction. Politicians at the time spoke of how the travellers had to acquire their own land in order to live on it. The catch being, when travellers started to do just that, they found that they could not in fact get planning permission in order to build upon it. Often, they discovered this retroactively. The apotheosis of the trap laid for travellers was Dale Farm. In 2011, amidst rioting and barricades of burning tires, the traveller families were violently evicted from the land they owned and the homes they had constructed were bulldozed before their eyes. A campaign to save Dale Farm attracted direct support from people whose housing situation was similarly precarious. According to the *Daily Mail* newspaper website, 20 September, 2011 :

'Hundreds of anarchists turned Europe's largest illegal traveller site into a fortress today to defy bailiffs in what they say will be the 'Battle of Basildon'. Menacing activists, wearing scarves over their faces, launched 'Operation Lockdown' to stop the authorities from bulldozing Dale Farm for a planned eviction this morning.'

Despite the solidarity, 86 families, including an estimated 100 children, were forcibly evicted from the 'illegal half' of Dale Farm following a rejected mediation deal from the UN Council on Human Rights by the Foreign Office. Their threatened attempts to reoccupy were met with broad punitive measures in the form of draconian legislation to criminalise such efforts and keep the intended re-occupiers facing re-housing in a prison cell for their efforts.

Although historically there are examples of local politicos making deals with dirty squatters, the central government has remained indignant at the self-determination of their subjects. Thanks to legislation dating back to the 1381 Forcible Entry Act and Wat Tyler's revolt, squatting remained a civil rather than a criminal matter up until 2012, when the law regarding residential buildings was finally changed after a decades old campaign by the Conservative party. Section 144 of the Legal Aid, Sentencing and Punishment of Offender's Act now criminalises squatting in residential properties, squeezing the country's 50,000 or so squatters into the remaining commercial buildings, or condemning them to live illegally. This legislation builds upon the effects of the 1977 Criminal Law Act, which created the infamous Section 6 notice that appeared on the doors of squats for three decades, and 1994's Criminal Justice Bill. Squatters across Britain are holding their collective breath awaiting the hammer to fall on commercial properties too.

This rewriting of the rules of the game has been part of a Europe-wide backlash that saw the criminalisation of squatting in the Netherlands in 2010, the legalisation of Germany's occupied house movement earlier in the decade and the temporary closure of de facto autonomous zone, Freetown Christiania, in Copenhagen in 2011. Italy's vibrant scene is embattled with Berlusconi's neo-fascist strongarm tactics, while rampant repossessions in Spain leave many squatting in the homes they used to own. Barcelona has seen a decrease from nearly 800 squats ten years ago to just 300 now, but with a corresponding growth in the number of rural squats in abandoned villages to escape repression by the polícia. The squats of Thessaloniki and Athens have been turned into impenetrable fortresses, locked into trench warfare and siege mentality with their beleaguered government. Ongoing police raids in December 2012 successfully evicted heritage squats such as Villa Amalias and Patision/Skaramanga. The neighbourhood of Exarchia (literally, out of authority) continues to pluckily defy the domination of the State, despite the crawling tentacles of development and gentrification sneaking in.

As Colin Ward states in *Cotters and Squatters*:

'What squatters seek, and have always sought, is security of tenure, and indeed personal security. However, there has been a marked deterioration in the public mood which enabled local authorities in the 1940s and again in the 1960s and 1970s to make creative deals with squatters, but in the 1990s led central government, relying for support on what it saw as the self-protective instincts of a property-owning democracy, to adopt policies which have had the effect of criminalising them.'

The *Guardian* newspaper estimates that 10%[1] of the population of the world are squatters. That amounts to 700 million people across the globe. From the favelas of Rio de Janeiro, alarmingly 'pacified' in the run-up to the 2014 World Cup, to the sprawling townships of Johannesburg, to the sweltering tropical slums of Bombay, squatting is a global phenomenon that still provides one of the most direct and earnest challenges to the dominion of wealth and power. These occupied zones, be they in Palestine or Pimlico, are the frontline in the struggle between the people who live there and policy-makers who would carve up their homes on a map and share the spoils between themselves.

---

[1]   http://www.theguardian.com/society/2012/dec/03/
        squatters-criminalised-not-home-stealers

PART ONE

How Not to Squat

The desire to change the world remains merely an abstract ideal or a political program unless it becomes the will to transform one's own existence.

— Wolfi Landstreicher, *Against the Logic of Submission*

The shopping list read as follows:

1) Head torch
2) Gaffer tape
3) Toolkit
4) Yale lock
5) Bolts
6) Crowbar

We were a small crew of newbies, learning the squatting ropes the only way we knew how — through trial and error, learning by doing, progress through fuck-ups. I clutched the copy of the *Squatter's Handbook* (13th Edition) that I'd picked up at the Anarchist Bookfair just two weeks before. This bookfair is the biggest and soberest event in the London anarchist milieu.

Organised by the good folks at Freedom Bookshop[1], for one day each autumn, the hallways of the Queen Mary University in Mile End are packed with hundreds of crusties, activists and renegade wannabes. The winding corridors and lecture halls are crammed with stalls touting a rebel canon of self-published books, homemade stencils and vegan fodder whilst workshops on everything from the practise of consent in sexual relationships, international solidarity, dealing with police and the courts to queer anarchist history and seedbombs.

I'd been to the Practical Squatters evening at 56a Infoshop[2] in Elephant & Castle and recruited a lively Estonian partner, Vassily. He was nearly a year in the country, working as a doorman at some West End hotel, and had been living outside

1   A radical bookstore in Shoreditch established over 100 years ago by Peter Kropotkin and Emma Goldman, home of the longest running anarchist newspaper in the UK, *Freedom*.

2   A former squat turned legal social centre that is used by various activist groups, including a bike workshop, seed bank, and bi-weekly meet-ups for people interested in meeting others to squat with.

the North Circular in squats teeming with rats and sour with the stench of blocked toilets. Like many seeking homes in London, he was ex-military, waxing lyrical with sparkling eyes and a thick accent. Though he never mentioned it directly, he made extra money as a cheap thrill for boy-hunting bourgeoisie in the backrooms of the hotel. He connected us with a Lithuanian student, Vitaly, who had been couch-surfing and sleeping on the ever-circling night bus route, perpetually clutching his camera and tripod. Vitaly sported a haircut composed of right angles and jam jar glasses. His surname translated as something akin to 'gremlin'.

Together we set off on a month of fruitless frog-marching around east London, exploring an abundance of abandoned properties to be found there. The Government itself admits to 635,000 empty homes across the UK, not to mention the number of empty commercial properties. Peering in through barricades and looking for the circle-slashed-with-lightning-arrow logo of the squat international daubed on windows and walls for hints of where to go, it felt like we were on some ill-defined treasure hunt. I'd take long lunch breaks from my job to trek through acres of dilapidated warehouses, disused court houses, and ramshackle estates looking for tell-tale Sitex[3] doors, mythical

3   A generic name used for the sheet metal doors and windows used by different security firms to secure empty properties. These are rented from the security firms by property owners.

open windows and elusive easy-ins. In one visit, we walked for miles in the rain and ended up on the fourth floor of the Ocean Estate, where my companion guilelessly approached a swarthy looking fellow who was leaning on the balustrade and asked timidly:

'So, is many squats here?'

The man nodded.

'So, would anyone in the community mind if we moved in?'

Without missing a beat the stocky man had stood up straight and revealed his Securicor jacket and walkie-talkie.

'Yeah. Me.'

Shame-faced but howling with laughter at our idiocy, we beat a retreat. As it grew dark that night we witnessed police patrols moving around the perimeters, hassling people drinking in the park and generally disturbing the peace — a grim reminder of who else was on the opposing team. Eventually, after weeks of clueless searching, we attempted a Halloween crack on a place Vassily had known about for a long time, driven by desperation to clamber up onto a roof in Old Street at three in the morning to try to access a disused record store. Perhaps we were tempting fate, or perhaps we thought that on such a night the police and passersby would be too distracted by the macabre masquerade theatre of All Hallow's Eve to notice two grave-robbers and a gremlin shopping for vinyl.

Meticulous in our planning, we'd prepared a gaffer-tape

patch to put over the window to catch the shower of broken glass. We'd been shopping in little hardware stores around Blackheath to collect the necessary goodies for our trick-or-treat mission. Vassily and I scurried awkwardly up a drainpipe through barbed wire and a burst of tangled thorn to a little balcony by the back window. Behind us was a looming tower block, innumerable lights illuminating our actions, watching over us like the Panopticon. Ignoring our exposure as much as I could, I became ensnared in the barb wire, my glasses tumbling from my face, disappearing in thorns. Taking deep, measured breaths, I unhooked myself, thorn by thorn. I peered half-blind into the mesh of spindly limbs and tentatively fingered around until I located my spectacles. With a deep sigh of relief, I clambered up on to the flat roof to join Vassily.

I had the hammer, and clutched it in one numb hand as we crouched together.

'On three. One . . . two . . . '

I smacked it against the pane.

It bounced off like a rubber mallet.

Instead of the glass, it was our nerves that broke and we tumbled down to join the Lithuanian look-out we'd left at the front. We were wired, half-drunk from the Halloween party we had dropped into earlier, and railing between terror and exhilaration at what we were attempting. The streets remained free of police cars, the night air empty of klaxons and sirens.

All we could hear was the low-pulse of nearby bars and the occasional whooping mating cry of distant revellers. Rallying ourselves, we went back for a second attempt.

'One, two . . . three!'

Vassily shattered the glass covered in gaffer tape and with adrenaline pounding in my ears I surged through the access, as the Estonian would later describe, 'like a bear'.

Inside, we activated head torches and tried to feel our way through the detritus. There was stuff everywhere. The place was a ravaged Aladdin's cave of modern consumerism — stairs twisted up and down into infinity, secret passages folded up within rooms that may have been giant cupboards, a bewildering labyrinthine network of tiny cubicles. The owner must have had a penchant for washing machines; boxes of old taps, peeling plaster and 1970s detergent adverts hung off the walls like flayed skin. Upstairs, the roof was caved in and everywhere bare copper piping was exposed like old innards. Most disconcerting of all, from somewhere inside the building, the dolorous murmur of a television was ruminating like a judge rehearsing his verdict before court.

Hindsight dictates that it was probably left on by the warden to distract and deter would-be squatters just like us. Reason urges that we could have stayed calm, tracked down the TV, and secured the doors. Simple common sense suggests that if we persevered, we could have taken the building. The hard part was surely over. But we were blessed with neither hindsight, reason nor sense at that juncture, only images of irate owners and combatative security guards ready to leap out at us. It was the first experience of the shock that sets in with this kind of activity — a deactivation of basic logic functions to be replaced with animalistic instincts of survival — all intelligence flushed out by adrenaline and fear. We were as green as grass.

Instead of keeping to the plan, we began fitting bolts in a fit of panic to interior doors, trying to lock out the TV noise and protect ourselves. The remnants of our scheme to secure the building diminished to a frantic scurry to block out whatever was producing that haunting chatter.

A deafening musical bomb detonated in my pocket: the Lithuanian was calling from outside, carrying a tripod and camera to masquerade as a film student if anyone was to pass. On the phone, he reported:

'There's a woman looking in through the windows downstairs.'

We froze: trapped, rigid with terror. The battery was running low on the phone. We dropped the screwdrivers on the floor. For tense minutes we struggled to breathe in the dust-choked air.

At times like this, images of prison cells and the sinister scowls of authority figures fill the shadowy hulks of buildings. Time crawls, only the pounding of your blood in your ears as you count the breaths and await the crushing arrival of disaster. I'd spent only a brief amount of time in the lock-up of a police station, for the youthful exuberance of drunkenly vandalising cars when I was still a teenager. The chilling sterility of the cell and the hardness of the lock-up bed were experiences I had no desire to repeat. Blazing with adrenaline, the imagination can spin out a whole sordid affair of arrest, being charged, and the agonising half-life of ongoing provisional liberty in a silverscreen slideshow of the mind, condensing the torture of months into seconds and depositing it directly into your head.

The phone blasted again, mingling with a warning signal of low battery.

'OK. She's going away.'

Vassily and I looked at each other. The wordless signal was given.

Abort. Abort. Abort.

We scrambled, packing up half of what we'd brought, scattering screws across the floor, leaving a bolt hanging off the inside of a door. We practically fell off the back wall into the welcoming arms of the alleyway. Grabbing the Lithuanian, we fled deeper into the late night chaos of Old Street — goblins and Vikings, witches and warlocks whooping and wailing around Shoreditch, shrieking unhinged mockery at us as we scurried away to anonymity. The woman was driving around the streets in a Volvo, stalking past us like a circling silver cheetah as we tried to saunter casually to safety.

Taking shelter in a backroad, we sat slumped around the camera and tripod, blinking in disbelief and trying to reset our pulses. A Spanish girl approached us, sitting for a moment on the kerb.

'So, you have a camera? Are you making a films?'

My heart rate had hardly calmed down. We struggled to make conversation with her. I looked from Estonian to Lithuanian, and realized with grim horror that I was the loquacious one of our trio, the frigging ringleader. I slipped into teaching persona, having been working at an English language school in Waterloo only the day before, and tried the classics of intra lingual communication: name, origin and intention. She was a student somewhere in the city, most recently of Zaragoza, Christina by name. The small talk petered out, bewilderingly trite after the misadventure we'd just embarked upon. She seemed to have something on her mind, which she eventually blurted out:

'Are you guys porn stars?'

There was an awkward moment of incredulity.

Then, we laughed, the incongruity of her supposition shattering the post-thrill numbness clogging our speech.

We were as green as grass, just trying to get a home-of-our-own, not suave-ass sexual adventurers on the make. Eventually, she tired of our lack of innovation in her evening's entertainment, and abandoned us on our street corner to ponder our ineptitude. Instead of becoming squatters, or even porn stars, we remained homeless on a Saturday night in London. Around us, the chosen ones of Shoreditch partied and pranced and laughed and danced, enjoying the transient liberty they bought with a week of work and obedience. For a moment as I slumped in the gutter, I envied their carefree revelry. For a long moment I considered capitulation. I could choose to stop resisting, give in to the pressures of conformity, of normality, to the logic of submission. They were big, organised, in control. Their strength was in the flashing blue lights and the shriek of police sirens. Their power was in the written laws and the tyranny of bureaucracy. Their dominion was everywhere, in money, in business suits, in the collective hallucination their domination convinced everyone was real. We sloped back down the Commercial Road, through streets that once housed tenements of radical workers, squalling families trapped in poverty and the most squalid slums of Victorian London, now occupied by glitterati celebrating their obsequiousness. Buckling and defeated, we went our separate ways to slip back into whatever couches, floor spaces or increasingly impatient friends' places could keep us off the streets that night.

As I crawled into my sleeping bag on my friend's floor, I reflected on what had happened. Despite our failure, we had taken an important first step. We were on our way to some alien destination that made promises of untold liberty.

Never Move to Peckham

All over the place, from the popular culture to the propaganda system, there is constant pressure to make people feel that they are helpless, that the only role they can have is to ratify decisions and to consume.

— Noam Chomsky

'Never move to Peckham.'

The woman in the queue at Costcutter had given us an ominous pronouncement, and my first eviction proved to be an ignominious affair — though later experience would show that few could be described as honourable.

We had tracked down some squatter allies — friends of friends from overseas — who'd taken pity on our plight and given us a key to a traditional squat on the Queen's Road in Peckham. The story of our bungling crack attempt the week before prompted a perplexed headshake, like an old man addressing a hormonal teenager. The first lesson of squatting:

'Never try to open on Halloween.'

To give a snapshot of the area: we saw three street fights in the first few days we were there, and most commercial premises seemed to be pound stores, thrift shops or halal butchers. There was a glut of fried chicken available. The area used to be home to lots of squats, as well as a thriving local culture with strong ties to one another, a genuine community, but speak to anyone who had lived there for more than a year's tenancy and they would talk woefully of how the borough was crumbling under the assault of property developers, hip-seeking urban professionals and the transient hordes who seek out the latest neighbourhood to acquire that debilitating veneer of desirability. Here, in later years, gentrification would replace the butchers and pound stores with coffee shops and, in time, that icon of ephemeral appropriation, the pop-up boutique.

Unlocking the Sitex door, our tiny cell occupied the shell on a rainy Saturday night. It was me, Vitaly, Vassily and a young Malaysian girl named Noodles. A terraced council property, it had been squatted and re-squatted by successive generations of people for over two decades. Typically, each eviction would result in more damages caused by bailiffs and owners in an attempt to deter subsequent reoccupation. There was no power, not even fuses in the box, no carpeting, and no glass in many of the upstairs windows. We left the Sitex sheets in place to try to keep out the winter wind, and even caravanned a toilet on the Tube to install in the devastated upstairs bathroom, riding our porcelain throne through the underground like hobo kings. It was rough, but it was our new home.

At 7pm on a Saturday night, a week since our rooftop folly, we unlocked the door and entered the husk. The first steps into an abandoned building are magical. You feel your breath stir the dust from a space left to rot, new life entering a dead place. We trod creaking boards like tentative tomb robbers, reading strange hieroglyphs scrawled on the walls and tracing our fingertips over the melee of paint that previous occupants had left like psychedelic slug trails. These were the only signs of life, loops of leaves and the giant screaming face of some forgotten deity shrieking quietly in the darkness of the stairwell, like messages from a dead civilisation. We peeked out of the broken windows into the wintery streets of Peckham from behind steel grates, spying on couples hurrying home through the drizzle, furtively watching busloads of party-goers off to New Cross or heading into the centre.

We got to work immediately. Noodles took a broom we found in a bin and began pushing piles of dirt into the corners. In an attempt to make our hovel more homely, the boys decided to remove the Sitex and install a set of bolts and a Yale to the wooden interior door. We had no idea what we were doing, no concept of the risks we were taking or the dangers we faced, stripping off our armour to enter the arena naked. It was plain idiocy to remove the solid and easily securable Sitex door, which formed a serious barricade to outsiders. In later years, these doors would be our first line of defence, defying crowbars and frustrating security guards in a joyous role reversal, that which had first kept us out could be turned against those who would evict us. But we knew less than nothing, and the only way we could learn was by making mistakes.

The Estonian stepped outside to fit the lock, and then suddenly jumped back and slammed the door shut. For a moment I suspected theatricality or horseplay, or maybe even a passing police car if we'd been unlucky, but I was about to enter my first battle to retain occupation.

A weight smashed against the other side as Vassily pinned himself against it, trying to get the bolts into place. I joined him in trying to wedge it shut. Each time the person on the other side slammed against the door it bulged inwards, held in place by a single buckling bolt — the last vestige of safety between us and whatever was trying to blast its way inside. Pressed against it and timing with the regular barrages, we tried desperately to slide the other bolt home.

As I braced myself against the door and the furious assault

behind it, I looked back at Noodles, slight and svelte, barely 20-years-old, standing just behind us with a broom in one hand and a look of incomprehension on her face. I couldn't help but imagine what would happen to her if the rhino on the other side of that door got through. She'd done nothing wrong except fall in with a crew of useless scroungers, and was in no way prepared for mortal combat. She moved to the UK to study drama and the theatre arts, her parents forking out tens of thousands of ringgit to educate and improve her, leaving her with a guilt-trip that meant she couldn't ask them to cover extortionate rent rates on top of that. She was trying to ease that burden, and better herself, but her noble gesture and her skills of dance and performance seemed suddenly woefully inadequate for the situation at hand.

It took three attempts before the bolt slid into the latch and the attacker meekly relinquished his assault on the door. Instead he shoved his flashlight in the letterbox and began a wailing litany:

'You can't stay here. It's dangerous. It's a condemned building.'

Maybe so, but it was ours. Gibbering and excited, I yelled the squatter's hymn back at him, right out of the handbook:

'We didn't damage anything getting in here. We have legally occupied the building. It is now a civil dispute between us and the owner to be settled in court.'

And as an afterthought, I added:

'Besides, you busted one of our locks! I'll see you arrested for criminal damage mate, not us!'

I carried on shouting like this until the Estonian delicately told me to shut the fuck up.

The police arrived shortly, and we spoke to them through the letterbox, informing them that we did not have to answer any questions as we were not under arrest or caution, and as we had damaged nothing on entry we were only obliged to deal with the owners of the house, the matter remaining a civil dispute.

'How long have you been in here?' asked a WPC through the slat.

'I don't have to answer that as we are not under arrest or caution,' I repeated, sticking to my lines.

'Well, I can tell you, you've been in here about twenty minutes.'

'Well, that's entirely your opinion, officer.'

It seemed unbelievable, but the police and the security guard left, flummoxed by the intricacies of the English legal system and a 700-year-old tradition defending the rights of tenants, and therefore squatters, meaning that such disputes are not a criminal matter, but a civil or business dispute to be resolved in a county court. Swooning with relief, we quickly fitted more locks and secured as best we could.

The first night's excitement over, we settled in to preparing the house — fixing the plumbing and repeatedly visiting the

Advisory Service for Squatters[1] in Angel Alley to try to get fuses that fit. There were several embarrassing phone calls to the extremely experienced staff in the ASS, revealing our complete lack of knowledge of electricity and eliciting enraged statements from the desperately over-worked volunteers:

'Yes, of course you need a fucking electricity tester.'

Despite our teething difficulties, we were a happy crew, ecstatic at having a home at last. The Estonian gave me his Calvin Klein glasses when my old pair collapsed in a mess of screws and lenses. Even though our prescription was different, they worked well enough. I found out later that the incongruity of a squatter in CKs often attracted comment, which is probably why he gave them away. We gave ourselves a name — the White Rhino Crew — after a local gym, though in hindsight it sounds like a South African neo-Nazi group. Our gang sign was a thumb pressed to the nose with a little finger protruding out in imitation of a rhino horn. Fuelled by Red Stripe and fried chicken, we clumsily worked with our shitty tools to remove the Sitex, taking up to an hour to pry the bolts out of each one and bring the massive steel frames crashing down into the floorboards, much to the distress of the council tenant living in the basement below us. We did

---

1   A charity run by volunteers, established by squatters in the 1970s, which prepares court papers and offers advice to squatters. Its offices are located in the premises owned by Freedom Bookshop in Whitechapel.

our best to keep quiet, but an uncarpeted, unfurnished shell of a house has much in common with a bass drum, and the poor guy must have begun to relish the days when it was all empty above him. Still, who would want to live beneath something as dangerous and condemned as our little home?

Fortunately for him, after just another six days of trying to find a fuse that fit, cardboard to shove in the gaping window frames, and sleeping at night with a candle burning on the wooden floor to give the illusion of heating, we were evicted.

Salty and grim after eight hours working with the children of Russian oligarchs and Saudi princes, I returned home and tried my key in the Yale, only to find that it spun around without any grip. There was no one in. The door was screwed shut. We had explicit instructions not to leave the building unoccupied, but obviously someone — indeed everyone — had gone out. Our little crew were all workers and students, people trying to make their way in the world. A great example of why squatting is a full-time occupation; we still wanted to work, to participate in the world, not shut ourselves away in our barren hovel. At some point our burrow had to be left unoccupied and that meant we were taking a big risk. We broke one of the cardinal rules of squatting, enshrined in the Section 6[2] that stated: at least one

---

[2]   Section 6 is a piece of legislation, printed out and often stuck to the door or window of squatted buildings that states clearly that it is a criminal offence to attempt to enter the building without the permission of the occupiers.

person is in occupation of this building at all times.

All our worldly possessions were entombed inside. With a façade of collected cool, I rushed down to the poundshop and bought a set of screwdrivers with the last quid in my pocket, returning to meekly find that they could get no purchase on the screws in the door. The futility of it was maddening, like a dog scraping at the locked door of his kennel. Dejected, I slumped upon the doorstep, head in my hands.

At that moment, the Sitex security van pulled up, and two workmen jumped out, looking curiously at me.

'Did you used to live here?'

I must have looked utterly pathetic as the November rain began to fall, and the workmen agreed to let me get our stuff out. Using a power drill, the headman unscrewed the door and I swept through, running back and forth dumping all our possessions into the street as they methodically swept through the house reattaching the Sitex sheets that had taken us hours to pry loose in a matter of minutes — binbags of clothes, a Casio synthesiser, an inflatable mattress, sleeping bags blossoming on the pavement like a bizarre fungal growth.

At one point I found myself alone in a room with the bunch of Sitex keys left on one side — a treasure trove of possible

It is not legally required to display it, but often it is as effective a deterrent as a Sitex door at keeping unwanted intruders out. There is a copy at the beginning of this book.

buildings to occupy — but I was so panicked and stressed that lifting them seemed too perilous a gamble.

As I lifted the last of the bags out into the rain, I paused in the hallway.

'Is it alright if I take my locks off the door?'

The workman shook his head.

'I've already let you do way more than I'm supposed to.'

The other one was more understanding.

'You can just get back in once we've gone.'

Our shitty-but-precious tools disappeared, no doubt snatched by whoever screwed the door shut. As they refitted the Sitex door I sat on the stoop and smoked in the rain, looking dejectedly at our meager possessions. The van drove away, and I was left on the street to break the news to the rest of our crew that we were once again homeless.

A Womb Without a View

This is a new form of sociality that can be brought into existence here and now in struggle against the order of domination . . . On the basis of these relationships of affinity, real projects that reflect the desires and aims of the individuals involved, rather than simply a feeling that one must do something, can develop. Whether the project is a squat, a sharing of free food, an act of sabotage, a pirate radio station, a periodical, a demonstration, or an attack against one of the institutions of domination, it will not be entered into as a political obligation, but as a part of the life one is striving to create, as a flowering of one's self-determined existence. And it is then and only then that its subversive and insurrectional potential blossoms.

— Wolfi Landstreicher, *Against the Logic of Submission*

We woke to the scream of angle-grinders on the floor above. It approached at ominous intervals, moving closer and closer, until eventually it was directly above our tiny burrow — a two level unit in the base of a mighty tower block. Minutes later, as water began to stream down through the electrical sockets and pour off of the naked light bulbs, we knew it was over.

*

Barely two months since a guerilla cell of anarchists, activists and homeless descended on the ground floor of the King's Court tower block in Manor House, the experiment in mass squatting concluded with a litany of grossly illegal practices and a shocking lack of humanity. For those two moons, over two-dozen people had been housed in the ten little apartments at the root of the mostly deserted tower of flats — vital shelter in the midst of a wet and frosty winter. The brutalist blocks had remained at less than 5% occupancy for five years, awaiting either council renovation or demolition, but for two months the ground floor at least was alive and buzzing with community. The few holdout residents above had been used as an excuse for the delay in completing a project to build yet more luxury homes in the area, continuing the gentrification of Hackney and Tower Hamlets and further pricing people out of affordable housing in London.

The water pipes in the floor above were cut either by builders or by representatives of Hackney Homes after a month of skirmishes and counter-attacks from both sides — a gambit that was tantamount to attempted murder. Once cut, the water pissed down through the ceilings, dripped off light bulbs still illuminated and flooded the fuse box. In a panic we had pulled plugs and cut the power to prevent our imminent execution by electrocution.

Under threat of eviction, the flats evolved crude fortifications — barricades lining the courtyard in front of the homes and double-locked steel doors at either end. To avoid the lengthy and repetitious hassle of legally taking the occupiers of each flat to court, Hackney Homes and the Metropolitan Police had succeeded in securing an anti-social behavior order on the entire occupied area, making it a criminal offence for anyone who was not a licensed tenant to be present there after 10am on the 4th of December. The justification was that the occupiers had been a noise nuisance whilst removing concrete breezeblocks that had been placed over the windows of most of the flats — renovations that had taken place during working hours and with the utmost possible respect to the few remaining tenants in the floors above. The morning the pipes were cut was the deadline for unlawful occupiers to depart — a notable coincidence. The builders had been working on renovating flats in the other block — one not covered by the ASBO — and became incensed after friends of ours legally occupied two flats that had their Sitex doors left open. The resulting showdown culminated in the police, Hackney Homes and the builders colluding to lock the occupiers inside — ostensibly kidnapping and holding them prisoner — until they agreed to depart.

During this situation created by police, security guards and representatives of the bureaucracy, I was in attendance as a wandering paralegal, jauntily bedecked in a trilby with peacock feathers, brandishing a bundle of paperwork challenging the legitimacy of law in this situation and a bag of fried fish and chips for the besieged. A mob of uniformed men blocked the narrow balconies, preventing access, but I was able to query one officer on the legitimacy of authority without consent. His argument: 'that the police and government ruled at the consent of the people.' My response — that I was 'the people' and that I was revoking said 'consent.'

Meanwhile, the besieged were reduced to drinking skipped juice they brought with them and improvising toilets. Noodles had to piss on the floor, unable to reach the sink the boys were using, something I'm guessing she never told her parents about back in Malaya. After seven hours they decided to call it off, abandoning their piss-drenched flats. They were released, passing through attack dogs and security guards with guaranteed safe passage, to return to the main residences downstairs and a soggy bag of fried fish and potato that I brought along as compensation.

*

I arrived a few weeks after they opened, the day after Peckham ejected us. Vitaly and Vassily took off to their respective safe-houses, and I realized with grim discrimination that their awkward Soviet charms would be a hindrance in my next desperate move to find housing. Explaining to them the situation, I set out to Manor House to try to beg a space for myself and Noodles. Perhaps in time they would be able to come in too. It didn't feel right, splitting the White Rhino Crew like that, but as I was to learn all too well, needs must when the devil rides. And we needed a place to live.

The November rain pissed down. I gained access through the Sitex front door at the base of the twelve-storey juggernaut of concrete, sneaking in as someone came out. Floor after floor rose into the grimy clouds, each one bricked up with heavy blocks of grey stone. Inside, I met the distrustful gaze of the occupiers and laid myself vulnerable before them. Typical of most squats, they were cautious but open, understanding my plight and obvious desperation all too well. Those I met said that if I wanted to stay I could go around and ask. Dutifully, I went door-to-door — dripping and morose but trying to stay upbeat. I had to sell myself, show those I met I could be an asset, not a liability, that I was normal and trustworthy, unafflicted by addiction or insanity, unlikely to explode and cut loose with a knife if they took me in. A Latvian builder, who looked like he'd just slung his broadsword over the hearth after butchering peasants near Riga, growled they were full; a well-spoken French literature graduate apologised with a sweet smile; a coddle of Hungarian rudies tinkering with a sound system were gruffly dismissive. Then, the door was opened by a mild-mannered photographer, who invited us in out of the rain for tap water out of empty wine bottles and jars of plastic humus. Flip was sympathetic, and still moving between two squats when he let me in. He agreed to temporarily allow us to squat-sit while he and his crew were moving, and the fixture became as permanent as permanent can be in squat world.

Flip was out of the Bristol squat crew. From how he described it, they were a much more pleasure-seeking posse than the tribes of London. Subsequent visitors from the Somer-squats would confirm that the place was awash with ketamine and turbocharged cheap cider. He and his mate had devised an elaborate rig and pulley system for ferrying joints across their dilapidated terrace bedroom. He moved to London to study photography, his portfolio extensively taking in the desolate wastes of abandoned buildings and the sweeping vistas of crumbling urban jungle around them. He was sweet natured, with piercing blue eyes, and a wit that kept our meetings jolly to the point of tears.

His squat mate was Tanya, a roller-derbying Aussie free-love queen who had a high position in a charitable firm and an uncanny ability at mediation. She interviewed me over the phone after we first crashed into the King's Court, appearing three days later with a mass of red dreadlocks and piercings to flirt her way outrageously through our first meeting. She is one of the most successful advocates of free love that I've ever met, skillfully balancing the needs, emotions and egos of multiple lovers and erotic situations with tact, grace and sensuality. At one of our first party nights in the flat, we ended up watching her get fingered to furious climax through a pair of ripped tights on a collapsing Ikea sofa by a consort from the local polyamory group. Tanya was the hub of the social cohesion of the King's Court, tirelessly communicating with police, security guards, Hackney Homes, and the various disparate squads of squatters who occupied each flat. Under her impetus, we organised English classes for the non-native speakers staying there, focusing on language to deal with police and authority, as well as combining our skipping efforts to share food communally between our crews.

For the time I lived there, the King's Court had the atmosphere of an outpost inside enemy territory — like a gang of itinerant scouts and refugees had combined forces in a crumbling North East London suburb. Hackney Homes was shelling out thousands of pounds on 24-hour security — surly skinheads with huge dogs and limited interpersonal skills who would regularly threaten occupiers and invade the courtyard space in front of the units. They patrolled the periphery of our home constantly, observing our activities and attempts to beautify where we lived from the higher floors of the empty blocks.

One night, despite living in lock-down, we made our escape into the wilds of east London. The Sitex door clanged open, our crew sweeping out into the dusk like renegade rockstars. Tanya's dreads blazed red in the dying sunlight, Flip took cheeky snaps and fiddled with his camera, and Noodles chattered and danced out the door, her eyes ringed with thick black liner.

We rode the bus down to Old Street station and headed to the Foundry, pointing out the tag of the Whitechapel Anarchist Group that had blossomed all over the neighbourhood since they'd occupied the building. Owned by radical dance artists the KLF, the Foundry now had its doors wide open for an open mic night of poetry and strange performances.

Inside, the walls oozed graffiti and the bar dripped with cheap beer being sold without license. Gangs of roughneck hoodlums, outcast pirates and sneering punks loitered and laughed lazily at the rolling cabaret. Members of the audience drifted on and off the make-shift stage, sharing their stuff and slinking back into the mob afterwards to cheers and jeers. A friend of Tanya's, a dedicated rocker with cocky mohawk and a face bejewelled with silver, pointed out a patch on my jacket — a stencil of a man breaking out of a barbed wire fence, and commented:

'That's weird. That's painted on the bathroom door of my squat.' It would be years before I saw the stencil in person.

Encouraged by the others, I sloped up to the compere and whispered for a slot. She looked a little flustered, but put my name down. Before too long I was under the single spotlight before the braying crowd. I was nervous — this was the audience I'd been writing for, and now they waited expectantly to hear what I had to say. They fell silent as I produced the copy of Howard Zinn's *A People's History of the United States* I had picked up from the Freedom Bookshop that week, and in a tremulous imitation of a barrister's voice, I read aloud:

'The prosecuting attorney, in his plea to the jury, accused me of saying on a public platform at a public meeting, "To hell with the courts, we know what justice is." He told a great truth when he lied, for if he had searched the innermost recesses of my mind he could have found that thought, never expressed by me before, but which I express now, "To hell with your courts, I know what justice is," for I have sat in your court room day after day and have seen members of my class pass before this, the so-called bar of justice. I have seen you, Judge Sloane, and others of your kind, send them to prison because they dared to infringe upon the sacred rights of property. You have become blind and deaf to the rights of man to pursue life and happiness, and you have crushed those rights so that the sacred right of property shall be preserved. Then you tell me to respect the law. I do not. I did violate the law, as I will violate every one of your laws and still come before you and say, "To hell with the courts . . . " The prosecutor lied, but I will accept his lie as a truth and say again so that you, Judge Sloane, may not be mistaken as to my attitude, "To hell with your courts, I know what justice is."'

The crowd roared with approval, slamming the tables and hooting. I was in, following up with my poem *Octogenarian Anarcho Punx*, my best impression of nasal Mancunian punk-poet John Cooper Clarke:

Octogenarian − insurrection − insurrection − octogenarian
No longer about just tea and cake, but smashin' the state
Never too late to make a revolution date
It's a fait accompli, see them barricading with their zimmer frames
Wrinkly resistance the name of the new game.
When you see them on the corner in the woolly bobble hats
They not leaning on canes but on baseball bats
Black studded leather cardigans and gats in their garters
At the given signal they roll them hats down into balaclavas.
They shuffle up in the bank queue, wait patiently in turn
No need to rush, when will the young learn?

When they reach the cashier, they whip the pistols from their
drawers:
"Get on the floor, bourgeois, and open the vault doors!"
Anarcho-feminist grannies, home-knitted woollens in red and black
Are refusin' their pension, the state can have it back
Organising autonomously at their annual organic vegan bake sales
They've learned how to live free in society's jail
They breaking their crinkly comrades out of the care homes,
Hear them making their escape by the sound of creakin' bones
Getaway cars race off − at 20 miles per hour,
So you've time to read the bumper sticker reading 'Fight the power!'
Grannies leaning out the back windows keeping cover
with the shooter
While Gramps rides shotgun on the back of a mobility scooter.
No longer marginalised
Their political views become radicalised
Too many times they been criticised
And their concerns trivialised.
No more hand-outs, or put-downs, or patronisation
Foundation − of the nation − can spark a conflagration
Temptation − to believe they can be cast off
But investigate their cocktail parties and you find they
mixing Molotovs.
So gather around children at the feet of Grandma Beatrice
Even with her arthritis she can make a fist

She got pierced nipples and a bright blue mohican
And she don't mind you peeking at her tattoo of Bakunin.
She'll tell you the tale of Alfredo Bonnano
Septuagenarian revolutionary, still good to go
He be jailed for his part in the Battle of Greece
But pushing 80 years old, still yelling: "FUCK THA POLICE!"
So, you down with O.A.P.s?
Yeah, you know me.
You down with O. A. P. s?

And the crowd screamed:
   'Yeah! You know me!'
   'Who's down with O.A.P.s?'
   'ALL THE PARTY!'

I staggered back into the open arms of Flip, Tanya and Noodles who ruffled my hair and smothered my cheeks with kisses. We toasted our daring, drank deep, and rolled back to the King's Court with a cocky swagger.

On the night of the threatened eviction, a callout was made, and reinforcements had arrived to help secure the flats, complete with booby trapped Sitex windows that would fall off when tampered with, floor-braces with steel doors clamped into place, and hugely dramatic wooden parapets that resembled the Omaha Beach landing defences. Among the reinforcements who turned up were a pair of old-school anarchists, speeding on sugar and adrenaline, hammering late into the night to protect the homes of others. They told tall tales of other resistances where they built trebuchets to fling parts of broken cars at the police and elucidated on the best way to take down a police horse.

'Punch it in the throat.'

'Nah, grab the bollocks,' his mate replied with a crushing claw-motion of the hand.

These two stood out amongst our motley crew, emerging from the night to show solidarity with those who needed it most. The eldest proudly showed two militaristic black stars tattooed about his collar bones, earned during the Poll Tax riots of the early 90s. Over the years, I saw more and more of this iconography appear on my colleagues, a physical recording of experiences and achievements, of loyalties and skills, displayed on skin for those who knew the code. Friends who could climb bore spider tattoos, those with light-fingers had 'cut here' and a dotted line just above the wrist, and always appearing was the anarchy 'A' and the tell-tale squat logo, stick-and-pinned into the crook of a thumb or behind the ear.

With gallows humour, these two free agents kept spirits high as we sawed and struggled to secure our homes into the night.

'What do you call an animal with a cunt halfway up its back?'

'A police horse.'

As people with obvious drive and confidence, they were hubs for others looking for direction, involvement, even command. The response from both of them was always gentle dismissal — these two were respectfully cautious of becoming bosses. True anarchists, they had no interest in asserting authority over others, whatever the situation. The others would just have to do their best, by themselves. In so many squats it's otherwise, with supposed anarchists easily evolving into the oppressors they claim to detest.

It was only when it became apparent that our crew was too fractious and too shambolic to mount much of a meaningful resistance that they melted into the night.

Our crew was a classic cross section of the squatting community — people from all over the world with a necessity to squat, organising together to make our little row of houses work smoothly. East European migrants, university graduates and working professionals lived side-by-side, united by a necessity for a place to live out the winter. A communal atmosphere reigned, with neighbours regularly popping in and out of each other's flats, meeting weekly for discussions and horizontal decision making, hand-waving our way to consensus under Tanya's facilitation. Daily, people knocked on my door with a bag of food and a kind word to share. Most poignant were the Latvian family who had been brought there by members of the community — a couple, Masha and Eugene and their eleven-year-old daughter. They were given the flat at the end; it was in the best condition, the windows unbricked and the furnishings largely intact. The family had been illegally evicted by their private landlord, and had tried all the available avenues to be rehoused, only to be told by the council, and by the charities, that nothing could be done. The squatting community took them in, and whilst in residence at the King's Court, they were unexpectedly joined by another.

Masha went into labour. No one outside the family even knew she was pregnant. The ambulance was called and a whip round organised for the family's bus fare back after the birth. Sure enough, she returned the next day with her and Eugene's second child, a little boy weighing in at six pounds three ounces.

Now we had a newborn living with us. We tried to explain this to the security guards who constantly harassed us with their dogs, to the bureaucrats from Hackney Homes who hid behind official personas, to the police who used their training to mask any humanity. We kept all channels open and still the order came — you must be out by the morning of December 4th. The family was moved to a safe house, a squat not under eviction orders, and the remaining defenders secured their doors and waited.

On the grey December morning of the 4th, many occupiers had already elected to leave — scrambling furniture, tools and other useful items into their vans and backpacks, then dispersing into the gloom. A van got stuck in the mud outside and a dozen of us had to wobble it out with planks and much colourful language before it could depart.

I remember the impregnable feeling of security inside our flat. The back windows were breeze-blocked shut, the metal sheets secured on all the windows at the front, and a twelve-foot metal stanchion wedged behind a Sitex door. Upstairs we had a heating cupboard that we left open and turned the place into a multi-celled womb of cosy heat where Tanya, Flip, Noodles and whoever else was crashing through would spoon together in perfect, complete warmth and darkness. Someone painted the blocks purple and orange, and a bizarre medley of furniture and carpet bedecked the place. Our snug firetrap — a hell of a lot better than sleeping rough. That night we drank bargain bin wine and talked ourselves up for the struggle ahead, sleeping as well as we could, committed to whatever might come next, secure in our solidarity and love for one another. Come morning, only a diehard cell of occupiers and volunteers had resolved to remain until the police arrived.

Behind the barricades, we held our collective breath, only to be awoken by water dripping through the ceiling and the mocking cries of angle-grinders. That morning, we packed our remaining possessions and left in the drizzling rain to find a new place to live.

We read in the newspaper a few days later that on the following Tuesday sixty heavily armed police troopers descended on the King's Court to evict the remaining occupiers — a 60-year-old weathered greybeard named Rudyard and his affable dog Cosmo. The procedure cost tens of thousands of pounds and hundreds of hours of police time, not to mention the ongoing expenses of keeping security teams in place at the estate protecting empty properties that we proved could so easily become homes.

Smash Down the Door

For the powerful, crimes are those that others commit.

— Noam Chomsky, *Imperial Ambitions: Conversations on the Post-9/11 World*

After the Peckham debacle, being evicted from the flats and nearly killed in the main floor of the King's Court, we were desperate, despite the brief respite and fortitude we found with those who had taken us in. Whilst other people moved in plenty of time to new spaces and places of refuge, we were still reeling around trying to locate somewhere to hide out from the winter. The friends whose floors we were back to crash on were sympathetic, but tight-lipped in response to our ordeal.

Christmas was coming, and people don't like to be confronted with the homeless when they're trying to get festive.

In the King's Court, we'd met an organiser from across the Atlantic. Ewan was a volunteer, a radical and self-proclaimed 'professional squatter'. He looked like a mule, all long dimensions and a gawky disposition, at odds with his agility and dexterous movements. When we first met we were begging a room to crash in and he was up a ladder, messing around with the sheet metal on the flats above, dealing with neighbours upstairs who were haranguing him and answering us in a confusing multitask.

'Shut the fuck up and go back inside. Yeah, of course mate, crash in the guest room.'

I smiled, recognising the accent and sharp attitude from the phone call about the electricity tester. He'd been a driving force behind the mass-squatting measure, pulling together 60 plus people on opening day to swarm down upon the tower-block. Ewan had big ideas — eying up the entire block of flats as potential squats to be accessed piece by piece. After our abortive resistance at the King's Court, it was his terraced squat on the dark side of Clissold Park that I headed to.

Shored up with scaffold, the tiny warren of rooms was crammed with furniture, speakers, tools and other bits that might come in handy. A couple of homeless Poles had occupied the other spaces, occasionally popping in to harangue us with the delightfully nonsensical and aggressive joshing of Eastern Europe. It's been my experience that Polish people are masters of spinning absurdity with an impeccably dry sense of humour that can leave the uninitiated in complete bewilderment but those who can follow the intricate thread of wordplay in stitches. At that time, I was very much in the former category, and greeted their surreal monologues with bovine incomprehension. Still, they lightened the mood through sheer enthusiasm. In the meantime we all squeezed into the frontroom, listening to pirate reggae radio from out of east London and chain smoking cheap Moroccan hashish. This was our base of operations as Ewan helped us plan our next move.

Two streets down was his suggested target. That very evening he took us to scout it — the Factory. It was not easy to miss. A monolithic manufacturing building, four storeys of gloomy Victorian masonry and grated windows, easily two hundred metres square. Directly opposite, a block of new-build flats looked down on to it, no easy access, but by Bakunin, it looked possible.

Ewan, for all his expertise, was also a stoner. The first night we tried to open, it was way too early, too poorly planned. Blasé, we strolled down from his house at 7pm with a pair of metre-long bolt-cutters shoved in a backpack, and spent a few confused moments peering at the padlocks on the factory doors whilst people prepared ready-meals and peeped at the evening news on their flat-screens in the building opposite.

'This is a really bad idea,' I heard him tell no one in particular, and we aborted.

On the second attempt, I was introduced to the wonder of climbers.

Certain people have been blessed by some hangover simian strain in their DNA which makes the scaling of great heights something of second nature. Such people can be found parkouring across the city heights for the sheer fun of it, or perhaps at protest camps scaling slender trees with climbing gear to reach the perilously placed tree-houses above. Climbers can reach those parts that other squatters cannot, peering up at seemingly impossibly high windows with the calm demeanour of an archer choosing her target. Every crew should have a climber, in the same sense they should have deft lock-pickers, stout breakers, shrewd organisers and entertaining fools.

On our second attempt, two people disappeared round the back of the building, leaving the spotters out on the street nursing guilty bags of tools. Within minutes, a voice came through the letterbox, asking for various pieces of kit to be passed through. Dutifully, we fed the letterbox whatever it requested — a hammer, a chisel, a pair of pliers — all disappearing into its greedy maw.

Up a dissected fire escape, four floors up an emergency exit had been left unlocked. Removing the bolts from inside had been relative child's play. For years afterwards, I would laugh every time someone told me that 'the window was open', remembering my own first attempts at cracking and believing it a simple myth espoused by squatters to cover their tracks. Yet my experience was to show, more often than not, that seemingly impenetrable buildings often have vulnerability for sharp-eyed squatters to take advantage of.

Inside, a maelstrom of collapsed tiles, rotting floorboards, cement-dust piles, towering ceilings and a huge lift shaft with all its gears and mechanisms rusted completely together. It was a mausoleum, and we delighted in running to and fro kicking up dust-falls like astronauts gamboling around the surface of the moon. Occupying empty buildings involves inhaling a lot of dust, I was learning, and the masks that you see on the Black Bloc most likely double as handy ventilators when moving the piles of mysterious powder.

Refugees from King's Court began pouring in in the next few days, fresh hands to help clear and prepare the space as the weather continued to worsen. Strangely, almost none of them had stuck around for the resistance, or helped with the opening, but they showed no qualms in turning up and seeing the potential in the newly occupied space.

'This is free space. This is squat,' they opined, raising the difficulty of living a lifestyle outside of the constraints of property rights. Indeed, we had no better claim to it than they, apart from the significance of 'opener's rights', also known as, 'finders keepers, losers weepers.' I felt uncomfortable in setting myself as an authority on who could stay and who should go, having been door-to-door begging for shelter not one month prior.

The sheer size of the building made it totally impractical to heat, so we began throwing up makeshift shelters out of tarps and scraps of plastic we scrounged from the surrounding area. Noodles and I made a passable living room in one corner, next to a Bedouin shanty town of tents and bivouacs. Like lighting candles on the floor of a gutted shell in winter, the room we built was largely for the illusion of comfort: three strips of Harris fencing[1] draped with a silk-thin cloth, the dusty concrete floor covered by a filth-encrusted Persian rug we pulled out of a bin. The Latvians from King's Court rocked up with a van of wood and knocked up a couple of private rooms on the upper floors, retiring to them to drink and shout merrily in that inimitable eastern European way of furious celebration. Our kitchen blossomed: an electric cooker, shelves, even sections for vegan and non-vegan. Someone knew how to turn the water on at the stopcock in the street, and also knew it was a criminal offence for anyone to turn it off again. We were set.

In the Factory I learned how warm it is to sleep under rolls of carpet, just the nose sticking out to fog the night-air above, and how making love in furtive silence in a room that is a single

---

1   Lightweight steel fencing used by builders to section off areas under construction found on most building sites.

acoustic unit can be a stimulating challenge. At the Factory I met two second-generation squatters in their mid-20s who had been born and raised in squats in the 80s and 90s, people who had never rented, whose parents had not rented for decades, who told me, rightly so, that it was rude to enquire about a person's second name. It was here that I learned to never change the locks during the day.

The neighbours in the flats opposite had obviously seen and called someone, and presented us with a gang of enraged Pakistanis outside our door. We were well prepared — a doorbrace of solid steel was jammed against a plank bolted into the concrete — and through the letterbox we listened to the apoplectic tirades of the owners of the property.

Previously, I had only been in council owned properties — the aristocratic Queen's Road and King's Court. This was the first time I came face-to-face with someone who was personally afflicted by our homelessness. Mr Juwari proved to be a most persistent combatant, obviously enraged and indignant at our occupation of a building he had left abandoned for seven years. He claimed he had left tools inside, but by the time I entered, there was no trace of anything more valuable than pulverised concrete.

When the police arrived and told him that there was nothing they could do, that he had to go to court to resolve the dispute, there was much shouting and accusation. By some strange, convoluted turn of events, word reached the police that there was a child inside, and in order to prevent them forcibly entering to rescue this phantom-infant, each female member occupying the space had to go to the window and declare they were childless.

First contact established, we went about our business, getting as comfortable as is possible in a derelict factory in the midst of winter. The vegans in the house insisted we must separate all the cutlery and the chopping boards, with nothing being used for meat to be crossed over into their puritanical domestic regime. Rudyard, the sole defender of the King's Court, arrived with his adorable dog, shuffling around in the gloom and upping our average age by a good three decades.

One night, the rain pissing down, we were interrupted from our efforts to pin a tarp across the leaking roof by one vegan teenager rushing up to us in panic. Apparently, a homeless person nobody knew had been let in, and was seeking permission to stay. Tanya and Flip had already departed to more stable housing with a resolution to rent once again. One fellow we lived with, a worker permanently dressed in the fluorescent orange camouflage of a high-visibility jacket, kind of knew the guy, as a Pole with a reputation for drinking. The vegan teen saw him as a ticking time bomb. Diplomatically, I tried to get the all-important vouchsafe.

'So you know him. So you can vouch for him.'

'Well, yeah, but no. I mean, I know him. He's a bit weird. But he's ok.'

'So you can vouch for him?'

'Well, no. He's ok. But, I mean . . . he's weird.'

'If you want him to stay, you have to take responsibility for him. Can you vouch for him?'

The guy was reluctant, refusing to speak the magic words that would absolve me of responsibility. I see it now for the macho, bullshit posturing it was — as if I was protecting someone from potential violence by evicting this stranger into the street. I had not been greeted this way at the King's Court, yet here I fell into a trap of my own mistrust and suspicion. With a heavy heart I asked the homeless Pole to leave. We sent him out into the rain to seek other shelter. The teenage vegan was relieved. In the end, the homeless Pole's mate turned up later that night and snuck into shelter unnoticed — another nod to how timing is all important in this game of who-lives-in-a-house-like-this.

For a week or so, life assumed a relative domesticity. Jugglers burst out into performances of maths-in-the-air, vegans squabbled with carnivores about kitchen politics, shanty town rooms were built and we cooked stews with electricity we had every intention of paying for. I was still holding down my job teaching, each day slipping into work a little grimier, a little dustier, my wardrobe ever more ridiculous as my clothes became too filthy to sport in daylight. One day, halfway through a class, a French debutante took one look at my rainbow-coloured sweater, my too short trousers and odd socks sticking out of mangy boots, and collapsed into derisive laughter as I was mid-sentence explaining the present-perfect tense. I considered tearing her out in front of the class, but perceived in a flash how I resembled a homeless clown, and persevered explaining the intricacies of the perfect tenses.

'Before a moment in the past, we use the third form of the modal verb have, namely had, and the past tense of the main verb. For example, 'I had lived in London for one year before . . .'

One lunch break, I overheard an older woman who worked at the school talking about squatting, and was surprised to hear that she had been squatting for years, and that she had just received papers on a place she had been in for nearly forty-eight months. It seemed unbelievable. In just two months I had managed to be evicted twice, thrice if you counted the abortive occupation of the flats in the King's Court. I didn't approach her for solidarity.

At night I would take the long bus ride home and pick up fish and chips and cans of Red Stripe, piling into the little corner of the Factory to wonder at the strangers who had turned up and installed themselves. Me and Noodles would eat greasy fingered from the fish-wrapper, watching a nodded-out heroin addict blowing spit bubbles on the sofa.

Then Ewan suddenly disappeared.

When someone disappears abruptly from squat-world, without warning of any sort, it's not without reason. Some discrete questioning of trusted sources revealed that 'Ewan' used to go by another name — 'Ian' — and that when these two names were confused he grew quite irate. Someone passed me the weblink to the Metropolitan Police's top ten most wanted. There was Ewan, wanted in connection with a some victimless grand larceny. No wonder he was such a good climber.

We lost a good man, a diehard anarchist, a brilliant organiser and dedicated humanist. I hope he has moved on to enlighten and enable other groups of the oppressed. I, and many others, are indebted to him, as we are to so many anonymous others.

We muddled along as best we could after his vanishing act. The drama between us and Mr Juwari continued in regular installments. The owners returned to try and turn off the water in the street — an offence. His henchman would be nearly thrown out for taking photos of us inside the Gee Street Court.

My first time at court, we shuffled in, near thirty people strong. Rudyard launched an impassioned speech against the injustice of it all to the golem-faced bureaucrat, Judge Stone. The judge let that wash over him, staring blankly from his podium, yet when our earnest but incompetent Italian advocate made several mistakes in his defence, Stone chewed him out as if his very essence and reason for being had been insulted. It was a valuable lesson, and I recommend to anyone who has any lingering remnants of the idea that such a thing as justice is available in court should get down to their local and observe the unstoppable motions of bureaucracy rolling forth. It was here I saw how modern courts are derived from the aristocratic gatherings once found in the presence of kings, with all the adherent theatre, pomposity and infuriating etiquette that goes with that. We were meek little peasants doffing our caps before the might of the judiciary, the very language and customs of that culture totally alien to us, beyond our naïve and outdated notions of 'justice' and 'fairness'. Our 'opponent', the prosecution, had studied for years and even taken an esoteric oath in order to join a special secret society known as 'the Bar'. We never stood a chance, but still we turned up, and I would do for the subsequent court appearances demanding the presence of 'PERSONS UNKNOWN.' The entire performance was like watching people filing papers away in cabinets; methodical and precise, with no real indication of the violence and oppression that comes from such paperwork. Stone processed us like he has done thousands before — with the cold mechanisation of a cog in the machine. We had no claim to the Factory, so we had to leave.

The possession was granted to the claimant, Mr Juwari. We took some small satisfaction that it was just before Christmas, and the bailiffs would be booked out solidly evicting old people and families on welfare over the festive season. The bailiffs were scheduled for mid-January, providing plenty of time for us to move on to our next space. However, it seems that justice was not a dish best served cold, for Mr Juwari went into vigilante mode.

He smashed in the Factory door — his own door — with a sledgehammer, which people inside managed to snatch from his grasp and pull in. The breakers fled. Whilst people stepped outside to fix the locks, the police turned up and politely informed everyone that they were evicted.

It was after this that I buckled and returned to the world of renting, totally exhausted by the chaos of the preceding months, ending up illegally subletting a room in a tower block in Elephant & Castle. Noodles came with me, and her friend from Malaysia moved on to our sofa in the single room we shared. Squatting whilst working and volunteering at an East End homeless charity had allowed me to save up enough for a deposit if she chipped in for rent too. Still, we shared three box-rooms between seven people — total renting strangers, devoid of the community spirit of the squats — but the door remained untroubled by hammers. Joy of joys, the heating worked. During the time we rented, the police still appeared, dealing with one other resident who'd had a total breakdown and vanished. I spoke to them through the security door, all my instincts to refuse them entry.

'Look, we just want to search his room for any clues of his

whereabouts.'

I hesitated, then let them in.

As soon as the door was unlocked, they grabbed it.

'And by the way do you know anything about the smell of marijuana out here?'

I'd just burned one on the balcony, not minutes before.

'No.'

The guy turned up in a psychiatric hospital in Merseyside two weeks later.

Living there, Noodles and I began having violent screaming arguments, driven to near-insanity by our sudden reduction to a crowded domestic jail cell. All that freedom and liberty, despite the carnage and evictions, was suddenly stripped away, and we succumbed to the insanity so common in those who are trapped by contracts and lack of control of their own living situation.

Afterwards, I saw some of the faces from squat-world — Tanya and Flip in particular — who had similarly been driven into hazardous, expensive, alienating but ultimately much more peaceful housing situations. I turned up to another court appearance, saw some people from the Factory — Rudyard and the second-gen squatters. When I told them I was renting in Elephant, they whistled, and said:

'Posh'.

I was sad to leave them, the vegans and the drunks and the Latvians. But despite all this, the relief we felt in moving on was as warming as the constantly running radiators, further evidence that squatting is not a choice, but a necessity most who are involved with would be glad to have an alternative to.

This was not to be a tenable situation.

Interlude:
Where You Kiss Ass
or Crack

'Either we are all addicts, or none of us are.'

The frangipani tree drops purple-and-orange blossoms in erratic showers down upon the banana fronds and giant green umbrella leaves. In Buddhist iconography, it represents rebirth, yet here in Malaysia, it is poetic shorthand for death. Beyond, the silver tower blocks of the Sentul development overshadow the little tenement neighbourhood of Brickfields — the traditional welcoming committee of Indian migrants chasing their dreams in the land of gold. From my corner-room garret in the upper floor of the Lost Generation Artspace, I can lean on my desk and peer out over a panorama of progress: the tangled jade jungle gives way to the ramshackle high-rises of purple and grey plaster, which in turn are squeezed by silver apartment blocks that blaze beneath a tropical azure sky.

On the lot just next door, a family of Rohingya refugees have built a shack of corrugated iron and cardboard, nestled between the papaya groves. They string their laundry under the tin roofs, and chickens gabble amongst the ferns. The Rohingya are just one of more than a dozen minorities from over the border in Myanmar that have fled to Malaysia seeking respite from persecution by the dominant Burmese majority. Over 100,000 are reported to be based in Malaysia now, but officially, they do not exist. They have no papers, no legal status, and are at the mercy of the police and authorities seeking a hand-out to buy teh tarik with.

'It takes an addict to teach an addict.'

I'd been resident in Lorong Permai — literally tranquil alley — for a month, and was already considering the family next door a permanent fixture, when one morning the bulldozers railed up the steep incline from Brickfields and blasted their meager shelter to matchwood. The family were nowhere to be seen. Even the chickens had gone.

Lost Generation Artspace was a renovated two-storey mansion at the top of Lorong Permai. It had been taken over by a squad of Malaysian art-activists — Chinese and Malay punks with hardcore t-shirts and a militant desire to push the boundaries. Mixing together Muslim, Christian and different races was already a bold move in conservative Malaysia, never mind the fact that they were a mob of unmarried couples. The space featured bars on every window and a grounds teeming with cicak lizards and the occasional passing snake. It was the kind of place where you might go downstairs to the gallery in the middle of the night and find someone silk-screening a hundred cloth bags for a local grindcore band's limited release EP, or awake one morning to find a platoon of giant cut-outs of the opposition representative being lined up to attend a demonstration that afternoon. The sidewall was graffitied with a huge stencil of a man carrying a pyramid of cardboard boxes from the apex upwards.

'Art is for everyone. We are all artists.'

The artists made a deal with the property company who owned the building, paying what I always suspected was a bribe to some anonymous bureaucrat, to allow them to stay. The company owned the building and the extensive Japanese luxury resort next door that was slowly being swallowed by the jungle. The resort featured a number of crumbling, windowless hotels, their hallways being claimed by ivy; an underground library, complete with shelving and the collapsed remains of a projection room; even a barren pool, surrounded by tiled floors where loungers once rested.

Through a friend of a friend, I secured a room in this hot-bed of dissent and artistry, joining in with their installation festival, where they invaded the next door complex and set up a bewildering display of artworks under the title *Bangun*. The word has two meanings in Bahasa Melayu, referring to the act of awakening and to the erection of large, concrete buildings: arise.

Nearly 30 artists participated from across Malaysia and the international art scene, transforming the derelict space with inventive and inspiring pieces: plastic roses painted pink sprouted from between the crumbling stairwells; a collapsed floor filled by hundreds of Lilliputian cement mixers; the pool area was invaded by hundreds of toy soldiers fighting a gargantuan battle across its searing ceramic surfaces. My own contribution: a six-foot wooden giraffe bedecked in an Acapulco shirt with a straw hat and sunglasses, a giant plastic clock slung around its neck, making its way across a room full of beer can cacti, beneath a paper-umbrella-sun adorned with a giant 'A'. My first self-portrait.

'Personal issues are social issues.'

My work visa read 'speech and drama tutor' and was sponsored by an elite private school out on the fringes of Kuala Lumpur, yet I spent most of my time either in Lorong Permai or in a little village about one hour's drive from the end of the commuter line. Batu Arang is a former coal mining town on the outskirts of the sprawling suburban wastes of Malaysia's booming capital. It is conveniently located near the Sungai Buloh Hospital, where the best HIV/AIDS treatment in the country is available. This means a large number of NGOs have rented buildings in the dying town, and moved in communities of the rejected of Malaysian society — Myanmar refugees, the disabled and disowned, and *sampah masyarakat* — the scum of the nation. Heroin addiction and HIV-positive status are intimately interlinked in Malaysia and carry a heavy stigma — more than 70% of people living with HIV are infected by sharing needles. After decades of bouncing in and out of prison, becoming sicker and sicker, they make their way through the religious-based rehabilitation programmess, until they find their place at the Welcome Community Home in Batu Arang.

WCH is about a dozen buildings, scattered across the village, each surrounded by an ever extending network of organic farms, fish ponds and groves of fruit. It is the passion and obsession of one man, Mr Alex Arokiam, an aging, white-haired Tamil revolutionary with a hand-drawn picture of Che Guevara on the wall. Mr Alex used to take his guitar down to the slums and sing Marxist songs to those he found there. Now, he works twenty-hours a day organising communities in the jungle, helping them to find work, purpose, medical care and shelter. He tells me humbly that they never turn anybody away.

'We are fallen leaves. We may not look like much, and we might be quickly swept up by the side of the road and burned. Yet these fallen leaves nourish the seeds underneath, and can help new things to grow.'

Each building features a cast of characters, marked by drug experience, prison tattoos, the trauma of seeking asylum. They share rooms and cook together, work in the garden, transport the sick and infirm to and from the hospital. Together, they sustain. Mr Alex sits at the centre of the whole operation, at times uncomfortably like a lord at the centre of his fiefdom, his worker-peasants bound and beholden to him.

If he is a dictator, he is a loved and benevolent one, and the devotion he inspires in those who come to him belies the alienation and rejection they felt before. The penalty for drug smuggling in Malaysia is death, but these simple users and addicts have often spent half their life incarcerated in prison or one of the *pusat serenti* — giant rehabilitation centres they build in the jungle. They are older, in their forties and fifties, and speak of a time in the 80s when the warrens of junkies around Petaling Street were cleared. Vans turned up one morning and all the addicts were driven into the back before being transported into the camps. This social cleansing made room in the centre for waves of tourists to arrive in the 90s with the completion of the international airport.

'I started smoking opium in my village, when I was ten. I used to watch the opium smokers, and think how beautiful the smoke was, like a dragon's tail. Now I am addicted to heroin. I am 54-years-old.'

Heroin is Malaysia's guilty secret. Most tourists passing through visit the twin towers of Petronas, buy some knock-off Gucci in Petaling Street, perhaps the more adventurous tripping up to downtown Chow Kit to gawp at the ladyboys, but few would suspect the severity of the addiction issue in 'Malaysia — truly Asia.' A registered 300,000 users, and an estimated four times that unregistered, means perhaps 1 million heroin users in a country of only 22 million people. It's my job to work with a team of a dozen residents here, using theatre and performance to create dialogue and exchange between group members and the general public. We rehearse every chance we can, playing games and making stories together for long hours in the tropical heat, the constant chirp of cicadas and occasional howls of birds our soundtrack. Together we explore why they turned to drugs in the first place, finding shared resonances amongst one another as each reveals how they wished to escape conformity and the restrictive controls of family, religion and state. Drugs were a way to rebel, to mark themselves as different, to kill boredom and create an outlaw identity. Often they didn't know what they were getting into.

Now, we tour the country by van, visiting schools and art shows to perform with people there and discuss afterwards how drugs, sex and sickness impact and effect our lives. We travel to Pahang, to Georgetown, to Alor Setar, up and down the perfect, endless motorways that scream of Malaysia's development and sophistication. We pass miles of rundown concrete shops, pristine new developments awaiting occupation, monocultures of palm oil, banana, rubber and coconut. We visit hidden junglecamps of refugees and talk healthcare, or walk the back alleys of Chinatown to look for half-remembered faces from the past.

'Those who are oppressed, oppress others to feel empowered.'

As they perform, these rejects are transformed. The games inspire frivolity in the face of bleak isolation from society. Community is formed through the simple act of throwing a beanbag from one to another whilst speaking the name of the recipient. A lifetime of pretending to be something they are not charms and entices the audience to cross the fourth wall, enter the stage, to improvise solutions to the problems of addiction, peer pressure and mistreatment that are presented. They are natural actors, and in post-show discussions talk humbly and sincerely of the trauma and seduction they suffered through drug addiction.

In Malaysia, drug addiction was once treated through humiliation conditioning. Addicts would be made to swim in open sewers, to wash the stain of addiction from themselves with human shit, to swill their mouths with it and spit it at each other.

Now, they have attained a dignity previously denied. Everywhere we perform, the stereotypes and assumptions persist: they are scum; they are inhuman. Yet through 30 minutes of performance and interactive discussion the actors humanise themselves, becoming people with reasons and stories to tell.

It rolls on for months, and I am blissfully happy, all sense of time lost to the lack of seasons in the tropics: it's always hot and wet. I am drug and alcohol free. I pass a drugs test for my visa and ring my dad to tell him proudly. I eat fried rice with chili and mutton most days, or steaming bowls of fish-ball soup, or nibble sickly sweet Indian sugar treats. Working with heroin addicts, I feel the same weird sense of displacement I had whilst volunteering at the Crisis centre in Aldgate. I was on both sides of the fence, both a worker and a client, both offering advice and support and receiving it. There, it was taking the register and working in the office, whilst squatting and struggling to find food at the same time. At times when I slept in the rehab centre, listening to the cicaks sing and fans whirling the tepid humidity, I wondered if

I was delusional, thinking I was something different, when in reality I was as much an addict as they were.

'Forum theatre is the first person collective pronoun: we.'

The idyll is shattered when I fall into a dispute with another organiser in the group. She insists that she is the boss, that she's in charge, and that she has the final say. I argue that we are all equal, that we all owned the group and the concept equally, and that only together could we make decisions. She stops talking to me. She issues my dismissal by letter, informing me that my services are no longer required. I nearly break. I could have packed my bag and flown home right then.

In response, we organise an open meeting of the actors and addicts. After much discussion, we occupy the rented house in Batu Arang and refuse to turn the keys over to her. We send out the van to collect more of our former members from where they languish in the trash-strewn alleys of Kuala Lumpur. We issue our demands; that we should remain autonomous, horizontally organised, and that she is welcome to continue to work with us, but only under conditions of total equality within the group.

'The group makes the decisions.'

The group persevere, pulling together to organise their daily lives and continue their outreach work. They pass a hat around at performances and busk on the streets. We even manage a degree of autonomy from Mr Alex, providing enough self-generated funds to feed the crew and pay the rent independently. Against all expectations, they hold it together without a strong central leadership, without a domineer. At least for a year more they continue, making their decisions collectively through sometimes endless discussion circles, each one kicked off by games and laughter, often with a medley of beanbags tossed through the air.

The drive from Kuala Lumpur to Batu Arang used to take a side road through a vast expanse of reserved forest. You could feel the temperature drop as you turned off the highway, the cool humidity of the under-canopy sheltering the van from the oppressive heat of the equatorial sun. One time, we went back that way, and behind the gigantic sign announcing severe fines for illegal logging, suddenly we saw the vicious scar of red soil. We stopped the van.

For miles in every direction, the virgin, tangled forest had been cleared, only barren red soil stretching over terraces and hills into the distance. The jungle had been stripped. The sun beat mercilessly down. We shook our heads in silence. Such was progress.

Afterwards, every time we drove down that road, we saw

hordes of hungry monkeys lined up along the motorway, their babies clinging to them, their hands toying with bits of trash and the scraps that passing cars fed them. Their home had succumbed to the relentless march of development, and what had been a flourishing forest had been reduced to a desert of rubber plantations. Now they sit, in families and packs, watching the cars driving by, waiting for someone to fling a bundle of half-eaten fast food to them on the roadside.

I heard that those who have heard the thunder, learn to hate the silence, and over the jungle the tropical stormclouds gathered and rumbled with ominous portent of the deluge to come. London was calling. I'd been away too long, and something indelible about my home country rang out in my heart.

'Jumpa lagi, kawan-kawan.'

'See you later, friends.'

PART TWO

Riot

A riot is the language of the unheard.

— Martin Luther King Jr.

It had been a double rainbow of a weekend. The seminal night of our opening party, I stepped outside into the Hackney streets and looked up into the dusk for a sign. Somewhere over Mare Street and Lower Clapton Road, the rain was falling, striking the sun where it shone from beyond Victoria Park, creating two, complete, perfect rainbows.

The social centre expanded into the toy store complex next door, a week of furious refurbishment installing a café/gallery space, a bar atrium and even a performance space, the stage built out of pallets with working lights and a little curtain.

The opening night had been a fundraiser for SQUASH — the Squatter's Action for Secure Housing — currently embattled in the decades old struggle against the Tories criminalising squatting. A hundred people — squatters, activists, neighbours and randoms off the street, had filled the space for a night of music, poetry and vegetarian food. The Saturday had been a follow-up fundraiser for a grassroots solidarity (not charity!) organisation in Malaysia. Sunday was clean up, and a little visit to Passing Clouds in Dalston for the jam-night.

*

Passing Clouds, like so many places, would eventually cede its identity to Shoreditch. It used to be an outlaw bar, before the regular cast of miscreant musicians and shabby locals were driven out by increasing waves of people who heard the underground grapevine whispering their name. The Sunday night house band — the Planet-Eaters — was a group of local Rasta drummers, fronted by a soul-voiced sufferer who wailed and chanted the crowd into motion in spiritual communion. The moods shifted between gangster ska, shanty roots and transcendent Latin vibes. A rolling procession of the crowd would leap up and perform, before slipping back into the boiling floor of rude and reckless dancing. I saw people struggling to keep up with the others onstage, being encouraged and carried along as they freestyled their way to harmonies unknown. At times sonorous bliss, at others utterly shambolic, it was a human quality we recognised and found charmingly familiar. What mattered was that we were there together, trying to dance out our demons. For every blundering bass player struggling to keep up with a rhumba beat, there was a leap-frogging Italian ragga MC, whipping his knees three feet up in the air whilst rapping ten to the dozen. I once saw a man there gripped by musical ecstasy. Storming the stage during a nyabinghi reasoning of drum and bass, he seized the mic like a knife and screamed into it incessantly:

'This is a false revolution! This is a false revolution! This is a false revolution!'

He knew, even then. At that time, for the rest of us, it still felt like an annex of our autonomous world, a place we could relate to.

Legal mischief-makers like the Freemen-on-the-Land used to meet there sometimes, before the People's Kitchen dished out tasty skipped veganfare in the afternoon.

Freemen are a group of itinerants who for a time confounded the legal system of the UK by interpreting all legislation as contract law, and thereby requiring consent of both parties. Their dogmatic adherence to common law and renouncing of their loyalty to Queen and country for a while would set magistrate's lounges across England a fluster with their trickily effective wielding of the letter of the law. A group in Merseyside at one time successfully seized a court in the name of the people and arrested a judge for failing to take his oath. We heard all kinds of wonderful stories about them using these skills to exempt Passing Clouds from such nuisances as paying rent, council tax or utilities fees.

Our mates worked there: forgetting to ask us for money on the door, at the bar, or ever. Eventually we had to remind them that they were supposed to at least pretend to pass money over, otherwise other punters got suspicious. We developed a system where we handed over a fiver and got five pounds back. Not thieving, just a nice rebalancing. When you don't pay rent or council tax, you can afford to have such a generous policy. It is conducive to the convivial party atmosphere so coveted by venues. Intimate, yet accepting of all. We earned those drinks, and never took more than we needed. It was all just that slight side of shady.

Years later, we were banished from the venue when A. headbutted a disrespectful security guard in the midst of a vodkacharged catharsis. Even then, the pronouncement was tempered with a postscript: 'at least for the next couple of weeks'.

Monday rolled around. I stepped out of the iron gates of the Well Furnished squat into a ghost town. I was after a pint of milk and a pork pie, but found only shuttered shops and a nervous atmosphere.

For a moment, I wondered if it was some kind of bank holiday. Listening in on what the few people loitering on the street were saying, I managed to piece together that there was trouble in London.

There had been action in Tottenham, the next borough over, the night before — cars burned, shops trashed, authority defied. An unarmed man, Mark Duggan, had been shot by police on the Saturday night, and London was responding.

Curious, I took a bike and rode down to Morning Lane.

The high street was a war zone. Wild-eyed youths were smashing in shop windows and attacking public transport. They kicked in the windows of Specsavers, and ran off down the road with armfuls of frames. Kids in hoods were tearing up the shutters on the pawn shop. A petrol station had been fully looted, its doors spilling packets of Twix and bottles of Evian over the forecourt. Police vans and jam-rollers were arriving, black clad riot police organising across the street. They formed a line across the road, facing off against looters who were tearing open the doors of a Tesco storeroom and handing out Diet Cokes to people. Undoubtedly, as the youth ran literal riot, the bigger boys were putting petrol in their vans to go clear out some Toshiba warehouses.

The police advanced and the rioters fell back, dragging bins and fences across the road to discourage an all-out charge.

Despite our efforts, horses were soon galloping through the streets of Hackney, pursuing ragged mobs of people who scattered into the alleys to fallback positions or move around to outflank the police.

Later, we rode our bikes over to Clarence Road to check on the Pogo Café — a local vegan/anarchist semi-legal. It was here the riot police looked really scared.

A car was burning outside the Pogo, flames rocketing twenty feet high from the gutted shell. The police lines were holding at various access points into the neighbourhood, preventing people from entering, suffering under a rain of glass bottles and bricks from the masked marauders stalking between the tower blocks.

I remember being face-to-face with one masked riot officer, stood stiffly behind a perspex shield, her eyes boggling with fear.

Two youths were overheard chatting:

'Yeah, you know what, I never did no crime, but after my cousin got stopped two times outside Morrison's and searched by police, just cuz he was a brother, then I think, fuck it, let's stop being suspects and actually perpetrate.'

I heard a startlingly similar story the night before talking with a guy from the East End. He'd been pissing in a hedge when a riot van pulled up and two police started giving him the once over. They searched him, found nothing, then made him get in the back of the police car and pull down his trousers. The guy was obviously distressed by this turn of events.

Two stop and search stories in 24 hours without even asking after them. It seemed clear to me that the riots were a response to constant, consistent, callous police abuse of powers directed at black and Asian youth in London. Though the mobs of looters had definitely been a cosmopolitan blend of ethnicities, Clarence Road was predominately black, and getting organised.

Right around the corner from the burning car was a child's rocking horse, broken, forlornly abandoned in the street amidst smashed bottles and shredded copies of the *Evening Standard*. In a sudden flash of inspiration, I grabbed it, and wheeled back to where the car was burning in front of the Pogo Café. A line of media-men, single-lens eyes flashing, were snapping what would become some of the most famous photos of the riots. I decided to give them a little show.

Mounting up on the horse, I charged the line of media, satisfyingly getting them to retreat a few metres as I advanced. Then I pranced up and down the line, answering their questions.

'I'm here representing the Anarchist Mounted Division!'

'What's the horse's name?'

'David Cameron.'

The media-men chuckled, and in the midst of raging violence, disorder and chaos, we shared a little human moment of humour.

A man in a mask walking past chipped in:

'You don't represent nothing, mate.'

Then another car exploded, and the sheer lunacy of what I was doing encouraged me to abandon the horse in front of them and flee back to my bike to escape into the melee.

We were touring around later, riot-tourists taking in the sights, when we ran into a neighbour storming his way out of the borough, screaming his head off:

'Those fucking cunts! They fucking robbed me! Cunts! Cunts!'

He was an old Boer and bore from Jo'burg by the name of Bryan, one of the subsidiaries to the Well Street centre. We called him 'the Saffer' — a nod to how few South Africans were in our circle. He was always manic, intense, maybe a product of growing up near the townships, dropping in often to talk tools and shoot the frantic breeze. He'd found the door of a local bistro on the lane open one day and thoughtfully invited us over to check it out and see if it was worth taking, on the condition he got to keep the sound system. We thought it worth a look, and strolled over in broad daylight to find the place unlocked and empty, just as he'd promised. Inside, we found the preparations for a refurbishment job about to get underway, and sure enough, after a week of surveillance it was full of a South Asian family undoubtedly gearing up to make their fortune. Bit of a liability typically and today he was more emotional than usual. We wheeled up to him, trying to get his story.

'They took my camera! They fucking took my camera!'

After a moment we realised he was beyond consoling, and some friendly people from the flats next door took him into their garden to prevent him from getting lynched. We rode on, with a stern warning to our Aussie mate not to take out his camera.

'No worries, mate. I'll keep it in my pocket.'

Osmond was a lovable rogue. A Sydney squatter, circus performer and all-round nice guy over doing his internship in graphic design, a talented cartoonist and juggler, always ready with a dirty laugh and sly quip. He'd gotten in touch through the couchsurfing website and impressed us all by helping to barricade the flat's access the first night he arrived. His mates resisted an eviction by stripping naked, greasing themselves up with cooking oil, and getting the bailiffs to try and wrestle them whilst they slipped and slid around. Normally reliable.

Ten minutes later, Osmond was being pinned against a wall by a large man in a black overcoat, demanding he hand-over the camera.

We wheeled in, four of us arguing and protesting that he would delete the photos, that we would leave immediately, that he had no right. He looked round at us.

'You lot are too educated to be here.'

A damning pronouncement, based entirely on the way we spoke, but it was clear we were getting out of our depth. More youths in masks began to gather around.

'Get their bikes!'

The Aussie managed to snatch back his camera, and the four of us burst away on our bikes, tearing down Clarence Road as fast as we could, not daring to look back. The others nipped through the carnage of broken bottles and burning bins, but predictably my own wheels gave a sudden hiss of deflation and the bike crawled to a stop.

Desperately, I jumped off, pushing the crippled treader out of the borough as quickly as I could, watching my three comrades speed off into the distance, oblivious to my plight. As I made my snail-paced getaway, I had time to survey the scene, and ponder what had happened.

Clarence Road's gangs and neighbours had established their own autonomous zone, effectively policing themselves, preventing the media and potential narcs from photographing people, entering certain areas, or even passing through. At the same time, people were organising welfare to protect strangers and kin, thankfully for our Saffer friend who had lost his camera. Two different but not entirely opposite approaches to self-organisation, manifesting out of the collapse of the usual social order. There was an atmosphere of retribution, even reparation, of people getting their shit back.

I caught up to the others. We decided that was enough action for one day. We'd seen a few other local anarchos strolling around, surveying the scene, but the possibility of developing this outpouring into a genuine insurrection was a step beyond us. We retired back to defend the squat, hearing rumours that the Tesco on Well Street was soon to be raided.

The next day, on page two of the *Telegraph*, was a full spread photo of a masked man on a rocking horse in front of a burning car, above a headline that read:

'GUERILLA WARFARE ERUPTS IN THE CITY.'

If only it had been so.

Total Shambles

If we don't believe in freedom of expression for people we despise, we don't believe in it at all.

— Noam Chomsky

The resistance at Clifton Mansions — a heritage squat of twenty years — was a total fucking shambles.

A social media announcement blared over the internet, and by the time we arrived at the building the night before the eviction it was overwhelmed — hordes of hipsters and thrill-seekers had taken the tube down from Hoxton and the East End. They had turned out in force to drink, flirt and piss on the death of a vital community in the heart of Brixton.

'Not an ideology or a conviction between them. Their brains

as empty as their glasses frames,' said Moleman.

He'd come down with me to see what we could do to help resist. He often railed against the hipster milieu due to his occasional, accidental, inclusion within it. His glasses' frames were milk-bottle bottoms, an inch thick, and without them his squinting, pinprick eyes could not pick out the miniscule text of the vast anarcho-communist tomes he pored over each night back in Hackney. When he'd drunk his fill of elderflower champagne, he would serenade us with verses of 'The Internationale' and other revolutionary songs. Eventually we would lose him to Berlin, but for now, he was solid among us in London.

We arrived before midnight to find a street full of fixie bikes and empty lager cans. As we shuffled up to the yawning gate and squeezed through the crowds to the stairs, plant pots, bottles of piss and flyers announcing the next all-London squatters meet up rained down from the rooftops of the mansion. Squeezing through the mob that jammed the courtyard, the stairwells, the doorways, seemingly every square inch of space pressed with sweet smelling flesh, we worked our way up the building — a four storey block of 1920s flats — to find the roof rammed with decadents. There must have been two hundred people on that roof, the chatter drowning out the sounds of south London beyond. People gathered as if at a society ball, clustered in groups, waiting for the quartet to commence playing.

After twenty minutes trying to mobilise them to move down,

to build a barricade, to shut a door at least, it became apparent that our efforts would be as successful as trying to herd cats.

Resigned to see if morning would bring a change of dynamic, we settled in to watch the madness unfold.

Moleman wandered off to chase some girls and charm them with his winning mixture of reserved English foppishness and blazing anarchist confidence. I stood and drank alone, not feeling social. I stared off the edge, down into Coldharbour Lane, where gaggles of revellers loitered and drank amongst the drunken detritus.

*

A lifetime ago, I rented a room in a place in Streatham, just a quick bus ride south from here. I was still working in Waterloo, before I'd decided all work was an abomination, and stopped off every chance I got in Brixton to wander the market looking for obscure reggae cuts and sucking up the scent of jerk chicken. I used to buy a Walker's crisp packet full of stinky, sticky skunk from the local guys hustling by the bus-stop. Back then I would even pay entry to dance to furious ragga in the Dogstar, or weird Balkan jazz in Hootenanny. Vassily used bring me there on the nights he wasn't working as a doorman, often ending up slam-drunk in some local flat, incongruously sipping champagne with some friendly strangers and sniffing around for a free line.

I'd drop into the Ritzy cinema and sample the dark beer whilst watching documentaries about Joe Strummer and Bob Marley. The Telegraph pub was smack between Brixton and Streatham, and used to host London luminaries such as The Clash and Linton Kwesi Johnson back in the day. I went to the reggae nights alone, none of my housemates wanting to drop in. I'd brave the bar, slipping through brazen rastas selling handfuls of weed inside, through crowds of people dipping softly to the DJ. I was never alone there.

It was a similar story at the University of Dub, held at that time in the Brixton Sports Centre. All down the street was the stench of ganja smoke, accompanied by the advertising klaxon: 'ganja-ganja-weed-weed.' I went solo again, determined to be a part of that scene, hungry for my first proper Brixton sound system.

I felt the bass in my chest from five hundred metres away, like approaching an exploding volcano, like the heartbeat of a giant. It only grew louder and deeper. As I entered, the very fixtures resonated and rattled as if the entire building were a bass bin. They gave out free earplugs, and I negotiated the rambling network of corridors and suspended staircases down into the belly of the bass beast. The gymnasium was ceiling to floor with speakers, easily thirty metres stacked on top of each other, dwarfing the DJ booth where dub-gods Aba Shanti-I and the Leodensian legends Iration Steppas were at the control. The sound was overwhelming, my very core liquefied by the boom of low frequency, shuddering up from your soles and rattling your organs. People swam as if in a sea of sound, unable to speak, stunned into blissful silence as they rocked and smiled, lost in the vibrations like pilgrims taking Holy Communion. I danced and smiled, was warned off from girls by an overprotective male chaperone. At four-thirty in the morning, the DJ dropped 'Jah Live' and I was evicted from my body into a higher realm of bass-bliss. I doubt my hearing ever really recovered, but it was not only that which was changed by that night. I cherished that experience, even if no one I knew could share it with me.

Years later the University of Dub moved to the Scala in Pentonville Road. It feels like a tourist trap or a money-making scheme now. Critically, they spread the speakers around in a circle, rather than as one monolithic wall of sound. Though I recognised the DJs and their sound system, after seven years that feeling of a South London outlaw community was long gone. Maybe I'd changed, maybe they had. Probably both.

*

Those days seemed a long way from where I was now. Still, it was making me nostalgic. I lived in Hackney. The boroughs of London operate as a monopoly board of memory — each tube station triggering a whimsical flood of reminiscence that would never occur until you abandoned that area forever.

After twenty more minutes of watching people schmooze and gambol across the rooftops, a haunting cry echoed out to me through the hubbub:

'Ketamine! Anyone for ketamine?'

I'd dabbled in the disassociative tranquiliser before, and tonight, it seemed somehow fitting to my mood that I would rather leave my body, and this place, far behind. I'd lapsed into a reverie for times long gone. I was alive. I was here. If I couldn't organise a resistance, I could fuck it up as adequately as they could.

'Fuck this.'

I copped there on the rooftop and scurried downstairs to find a table in one of dozens of empty rooms. I racked up arrogantly long lines, hoovering them up with a giddy thrill. As if I'd booked him to entertain my subsequent state, a chap with a diagonal hair-cut wandered in, and set up a pair of portable speakers pointing straight at me.

The disassociative state induced by ketamine has been compared by doper-guru Terence McKenna to 'wandering around an empty office building', which is, perhaps, why squatters are so prone to its charms. That night at Clifton Mansions, I had the inordinate luck to hit upon what seemed to be the perfect dose, not submerged in the K-hole, but ecstatically enhanced. The incomprehensible download of cosmic information and nonsense that followed is, as anyone who has dabbled in psychedelics knows, difficult to put into words.

It came on slow, but soon sound and light and physical sensation became amalgamated, nerve endings and sensory receptors overloading and swapping roles as the drug severed my connection to my body and allowed me to float somewhere just outside of reality. Invading hordes of miniature elf warriors marched in fluorescent carnival brilliance along a windowsill grown to the size of a planet. Euphoric princesses danced for me, bejewelled with galaxies, their heads ablaze with apocalyptic light storms, before melting into the floor. I tried to communicate with them, but my arms had floated off like barges down canals and my tongue made noises like popcorn cooking in a pan. Words changed meanings as I felt them trip clumsily from a tongue like fried bacon and become something entirely other. I knew, from somewhere far away, that attempting anything in this state was absurd. I resolutely sat cross-legged on the table and babbled joyful gibberish as a colourful pageantry of seraphs cascaded before me. Gods and goddesses frolicked through marshmallow waves of sound and colour, intricate psychogeometric resonances warping and coruscating around them. I splashed happily like a child in the mud pouring off the ceiling, occasionally vacating my body entirely and transporting to the land of the crypto-gnomes.

Time passed like cheese melting on toast. Just as it bubbled and turned crispy, I re-entered my body. The summer sun was shining outside. Many people had left. The ones remaining were grotesque mutants staggering and shuffling around an apocalyptic scene — the Homeless Shelter at the End of the Universe. My grubby clothes were smeared in paint, apparently not the ambrosia of the psycho-trolls but a can of actual battleship grey paint I had knocked over and proceeded to wallow in. The discomfort didn't concern me at that time. I was still numb to reality. My legs weak and wobbly, I toured the building. Several occupants had barricaded themselves inside their flats, but a stagger around revealed many locations left open. The mansions seemed to regress to a state of disuse before our very eyes — one last hoorah in the cadaver of a building that had housed the needy for two decades. Potent psychedelic chemical imagery was everywhere — one room full of burst pipes spraying water festively up the peeling walls, another hung with a beautiful *tanka* of the Medicine Buddha, apparently abandoned by fleeing residents. Someone thoughtfully started a fire in one room's corner, the antique timbers of the floor and wall enthusiastically taking alight. The incident created the only sense of community solidarity when a chain of people ran buckets of water from the bathroom to extinguish it.

The fire perplexed me. It took buckets and buckets of water from a nearby bath to subjugate the flames that had ingratiated themselves into the very timbers of the building. With a calmness that can only be induced by tranquilisers, I filed back and forth from the toilet, tipping water over the flames, reducing them infinitesimally each time, as though it were the sole reason I had attended the party.

Moleman reappeared through the smoke, smiling slyly.

'Ah, Mr Painty Man.'

Painty Man.

One phrase I repeated at length whilst enraptured. Moleman held my hand to stop me from plummeting off the roof as I weaved around, insistent that I was completely stable, and it was the building that was unsteady. The crowds of the night had degenerated into dregs. We chose to flee, scurrying out and back down to the Brixton station, but at the tube my brick[1] companion was pulled back at the gates when he was spotted pushing through behind a commuter.

Our escape route confounded, we returned through assembling police lines and re-entered the building. The gates were locked and sealed behind us, a weird crew pulling trash and furniture into the tunnel as we passed through. As a clear azure summer's day launched itself above the rooftops only a few k-heads and a band of diehard Spanish punks remained. We climbed up on to the roof via the scaffolding to watch the

---

1   Activist units are typically organized by 'buddies' of two, who form into 'bricks' of four, who combine to work within larger 'cells'.

invasion. Pulling up one ladder, we slung it down the back of the roof to provide an escape route if necessary.

Overhead, a police helicopter thrummed and scanned us with its thermo-vision. Outside a battalion of police, firemen, and even a special climbing unit assembled to storm the gates. Down in the courtyard, a man slept peacefully on a sofa, oblivious.

From the roof I could spy easily the roadblocks at either end of the street, riot vans gathered like grazing cattle in between, spilling uniforms and arsenal out into the cool July morning. Someone in the flats on the third floor had stuck their speakers out the window and was blasting a soundtrack of raging punk over the scene. Crowds of rubberneckers accumulated around the barriers, watching the forces of law and order prepare to enter.

They began to cut the gate. Some loose-limbed partier decided to bail, clambering over the fence and dropping down on to the squad of sappers below, resulting in the only arrest of the day. Despite his addled shrieking and flailing arms, the police quickly pinned him to the pavement and read him his rights. In minutes the works crew pulled the paltry barricade of bins and trash to pieces, cautiously treading their way inside. Sleeping Beauty was levered off his sofa and carried outside the gates. Up on the roof, the Spaniards began to sing, 'Puta policía! Puta policía!'

A single policeman looked up to the heavens. A masked

anarchist gave him the finger.

Moleman watched, his face inscrutable, as swarms of riot officers and bailiffs began to stream through the courtyard and into the building. He hung the Medicine Buddha *tanka* over the edge of the roof, lining it up next to some scrawled graffiti tags. In a deep, sonorous baritone, occasionally quivering in the wind, he began to sing an old protest song, over one-hundred-years-old:

Before the dawn is when it seems most cold
But as sure as the sun rises in the east, we know
That the stream of evolution is a constant flow
And the current evolution says that I should really go, oh

Don't you know that every seed, it wants to grow?
We can't stay underground forever
They can cut us off as soon as we begin to show
What they don't know is that the roots still grow

When the roots pop up, when the roots pop up
When the roots pop up, when the roots pop up
When the roots pop up, when the roots pop up
When the roots pop up, when the roots pop up . . .

But they can try with all of their might
To push us down to the ground but I know we'll be all right, right?
They mean to break my spirit through this exile
But I can use this time to further refine and fortify my style

The world that we're all living in
Is in need of a plan for the brotherhood of man
So, I'm off and running fast as I can
And the antidote I'm bringing is the pen in my hand, man

Don't you know that every seed, it wants to grow?
We can't stay underground forever
They can cut us off as soon as we begin to show
What they don't know is that the roots still grow

We're finally doing all the things we were meant for
We're finally saying all the things we should say
We're finally doing all the things we were meant for
We're finally saying all the things we should say . . .

We listened as they trouped up the stairwells, their boots a banging beat as we sang together on the rooftops. The Spanish punks stared and laughed at us, their haircuts like the plumage of exotic birds wafting in the summer breeze. As they neared the top floor we joined the flight. The ladder was still propped against the back wall, and by carefully lowering ourselves down we could hang from the ledge and get our feet on the top rung.

When the roots pop up, when the roots pop up
When the roots pop up, when the roots pop up
When the roots pop up, when the roots pop up
When the roots pop up, when the roots pop up . . .

Precariously balanced, it was possible to climb down the ladder, then drop ten foot off another roof, past some Brixtonites enjoying breakfast in a neighbouring flat, then down to the maze of gardens behind. Jumping a few hedges, we scanned for roving police, before sneaking our way through the back alleys to flee north to the safe havens of Hackney.

The mission south of the river served only as a lesson in how not to organise a resistance. Subsequently I met with other squatters from the scene, as far flung as Holland, who expressed similar disenchantment — an invasion of rich kids and the ragamuffin glitterati whose dedication to depressive hedonia had driven the core to despair. A familiar tale — those who would organise and resist submerged beneath a flood of pleasure-seekers and wreckheads whose ambitions stretched no further than a good time at the expense of others. The curse of squatting — a strain of nihilism streaking through those who occupy buildings with no further comprehension than the satisfaction of their own shallow egos by association with the rebellion inherent in defiance of the status quo.

I wondered what the point and purpose was, what was the best we could have hoped for in that situation. We might have held the building indefinitely, yet I had succumbed to the very same thrill of escape and abandonment, disappearing down the drugs hole when so much more might have been possible. Evicting 500 people would have been a massive and very public undertaking for police. Images of young people being dragged from housing by armoured officers is a startling image of inequality, decipherable even by the morning commuters staggering blinking and half-awake on the cattle-trains of the tube. Instead, all we got was some climbing practice and a bird's eye view of what we already knew — that they were better organised than us.

The 22 self-contained flats had hosted generations of squatters for two decades, including members of The Pogues and Turner Prize winner Jeremy Deller. Due to the ever-changing cast, occupants could not claim for adverse possession. As of 2013 the flats are on the market for 2,100 pounds per month for three bedrooms. I wonder if any of the party-goers who attended are now renting there.

Well Furnished

From: www.wellfurnished.wordpress.com

WELL FURNISHED WITH POETS!

Posted: June 17, in <u>Upcoming Activities</u>

Our first spoken word event took place on Friday 10th June with over a dozen performers taking the floor — including turns from inhouse comperes Katie Rogue, Furious George and the Ranter getting things going. Also tearing things up were English Al, John Richard Tyrone, Mel Tyrone (no relation), Flo Davis, Mooza Mohd, Steph Dogfoot, Charlie Dubfree, Ofir of the Turbans, Olah Nora, with spontaneous interpretive dances and jam sessions bursting out in an epic poetry session that ran from 8pm til 1am!

Sat 2nd July
@
Well Furnished
6-8pm Novelist
Stewart Home

8 till Late
Word Sound music
Have Power poetry
charity Event
Wed 6th July
People's

Be sure to check out our upcoming schedule with a COMMUNITY POETRY workshop on Monday 20th June, where we will use poetry to capture the voices of our local community, and the WORD SOUND HAVE POWER benefit on July 2nd for arts-for-social-cohesion charity Fallen Leaves UK.

Thanks to everyone who helped out and came along. It was totally bonobo.

Open Drop-in = Free Tea + Chat!

Posted: June 18 in <u>Upcoming Activities</u>

SAVE WELL STREET MARKET

Many local shops in Well Street, Hackney, some of which have served the local community for over twenty years, are facing closure because of rent increase of 200%.

These shops include several charities and have a well-established place as the heart of the local community. They provide affordable and essential services for residents who otherwise would have to travel much further for them, and they are what make the Well Street area a real East End community. The proximity of Tesco over the road means we get a nice talking point with locals — yesterday we were informed Mr Jack Cohen himself used to sell bent tins of paint on Well Street market before stepping up his game and opening up the first ever Tesco — named after his daughter Tessa.

Please sign the petitions in the shops and join the Facebook group to show your support.

COMMUNI-TEA!

The SUN sez — 'Tesco kills off Well Street Market!'

Posted: June 18, in <u>Upcoming Activities</u>

Off the shelf Tesco facts:

o They employ more than 250,000 in the UK

o One in every £3 spent on food in UK is in Tesco

o Every week they have 20 million customers

o Boss Sir Terry Leahy earned £3.9m last year

o There are more than 2,672 stores in 13 countries, including the UK, Japan, Poland, Turkey, Hungary, China, Malaysia, Thailand and South Korea

Sorry for increasing traffic to murdock enterprises, but they are doing a big scandalous expose on the demise of Well Street, perhaps oversimplistically directing it towards Tesco as the root cause, when there may be a more complicated and well hidden reason . . . beware of oversimplicity folks. Well Street Market's fate is surely part of myriad factors . . .

The following is from The Sun Newspaper, by OLIVER HARVEY:

WELCOME to the Well Street market, where barrowboy Jack Cohen used to ply his trade to hundreds of customers.

In 1919, Jack was selling his groceries alongside dozens of other stall-holders and did quite well for himself going on to found Tesco and earn a knighthood.

But now just three pitches remain at the site in London's East End, with locals claiming that a Tesco store opening in the street had sounded the death knell for once-thriving family businesses.

As Tesco announced a 13 per cent rise in profits to **£2.55BILLION,** street trader Martin Wiles blasted Sir Jack's legacy.

Booming . . . local traders blame change on this store.
Dad Martin, whose family have run a fruit and veg stall in Well Street for nearly 50 years, said: 'Tesco killed off the market.'

'When I started 35 years ago there were 50 stalls on a Saturday, last week there were two.'

'Just like High Streets across the country, a supermarket has killed it for independent traders like me.'

'It rips the heart out of a community. The difference here is that this market was where it all began for Tesco.'

Martin's pitch is just a few yards from where Jack, the son of a Polish Jew, began his empire with one wooden barrow.

Jack, then 21, used a £30 payoff from the Royal Flying Corps after World War One to buy a job lot of fish paste and golden syrup.

His 'pile it high, sell it cheap' sales tactic was a runaway success and he soon moved on to bigger things.

The name Tesco first appeared on packets of tea in 1924, a combination of the initials of supplier T E Stockwell and the first two letters of his surname.

The first Tesco store opened in 1929 in Edgware, North London, and by 1947 the company was quoted on the Stock Exchange.

Jack used to give badges to staff with YCDBSOYA on them. He joked that it was Yiddish but it actually stood for 'You Can't Do Business Sitting On Your A***.'

He was knighted in 1969 and died in 1980, aged 82.

Martin, 51, from Romford, Essex, said: 'Tesco opened a store at the top of Well Street in 1970, I can remember Jack came down to open it himself. I suppose he wanted to come back to where it all began. There used to be 11 butchers, seven greengrocers and a couple of fish stalls here. Now there's just me, a clothes stall and a butcher.'

Shopper Sue Williams, 68, said: 'I'm not old enough to remember Tesco selling its stuff from a barrow. But I remember when this street was full of stalls and was a proper East End market.

'All the banter's gone. It's sad.'

But Tesco insist their popularity shows they are giving shoppers what they want.

Chief executive Sir Terry Leahy has strongly refuted claims that the huge success of supermarkets is killing the High Street.

He said: 'When a Tesco store opens, shops around it do better rather than worse.'

He said people will come into a town where a Tesco has opened and will then stay and visit the local shops.

Sir Terry added: 'It is up to the customers to decide whether we grow or whether we shrink.'

But from his stall in the shadow of Tesco in Well Street, Martin stares forlornly down the road.

The market stalls are gone, replaced by fast-food joints.

WELL
Furnished
Luiz 8pm
Gabriel, Tonight
Lopes, FREE
Brazilian Folk
Poetry hippy Guitar tunes
Open Mic

The People's Banquet
Today!
from 5:30
Food 6:30-9:00
musicians storytellers & poets
Bring what you can
Free!
xx

QUEER TANGO

Posted: July 21, in **<u>Up Coming Activities</u>**

QUEER TANGO — come and learn to dance! Queer Tango is about intimacy, connection, leading and following, not getting stuck in gendered roles . . . all ages, genders, sexualities welcome. wear comfortable clothes and shoes that don't grip the floor. email for more info

::: MOVIE NIGHT :::

Posted: July 23, in Uncategorized

Come & join us for an Evening of :::MOVIE::: entertainment

We have a projector, surround sound, & are more than happy to screen Movies / Documentaries / Education Videos etc or bring something along, & we will consider playing it on the BIG screen!

We can also cater to groups; Tea's, Coffee's & Movie Munchies for your dining pleasure

+ Smoking area & chill Garden space relax

'Hakuna Matata'
(No Worries)

*All for **FREE** ~ (Donations are appreciated & will be given to a local charity)

~ Harmonic Om'ing Sound Bath Circle ~

Posted: July 23, in **Home, Up Coming Activities**

:::YOGA:::

Mind

Body

Spirit

{{{{~8~}}}}

*Drop-in One-On-One Yogic rejuvination classes available,

here @ Well Furnished, Homerton.

Please e-mail for more information.

{{{:::}}} Sacred Geometry Mandala Artist {{{:::}}}

{{{:::}}} Sound Harmonic Energy Body Healer {{{:::}}}

::: Harmonic Om'ing Sound Bath Circle :::

- Friday 5th August @ 3:33pm

<3 T'Om LOVE <3

Namaste

August 17th-26th Schedule

Posted: August 17, in **Up Coming Events**

We've got a jampacked couple of weeks ahead with the arrival of the Sonic Arts international exchange programme, where we have 15 international sound artists workshopping and performing from the 24th, the **QUEER CABARET** on the 19th, and the return of **WORD SOUND HAVE POWER IV** on the bank holiday weekend.

If you haven't been, you must come to check out our converted toy shop space, where we've built our own stage, theatre, bar and restaurant and serve delicious veggie food at a knockdown price. All donations go to community projects, so come and have a look before they make it all illegal . . . :-)

Wednesday 17th August

1-7pm — Drop-in sessions and open day
8pm — Poledancing workshop

Friday 19th August

8pm — ***QUEER CABARET***..polysexualgendertypedefying poetry and spoken word with the cream of London's performers . . . hosted by Katie Rogue, donation entry. 18+

Saturday 20th August

1-7pm — Drop-in sessions and open day
1-7pm — **Bike workshop drop-in** session. Learn how to repair, build, and maintain your beloved bike!

Monday 22st August

8pm — Queer Tango classes. Come twirl the night away in our romantic bed shop! No experience necessary.

Wednesday 24rd August

1-7pm — Drop-in sessions and open day

Thursday 25th August

1-6pm — ***SONIC ARTS FESTIVAL*** Workshop day in audio engineering and audio arts. All welcome, drop-in sessions.

Friday 26th August

1-6pm — ***SONIC ARTS FESTIVAL*** Workshop day in audio engineering and audio arts. All welcome, drop-in sessions.

8pm-late — ***SONIC ARTS FESTIVAL*** Performances and presentations from the festival, vegetarian food in our lovely Conscious Cafe space.

Saturday 27th August

1-6pm – ***SONIC ARTS FESTIVAL*** Workshop day in audio engineering and audio arts. All welcome, drop-in sessions.

8pm-late — ***WORD SOUND HAVE POWER IV — SONIC ARTS FESTIVAL vs REBOOT THE ROOTS***

Performances and presentations, vegetarian food in our lovely Conscious Cafe space. Benefit night, all donations to RtR.

Featuring Furious George MC (UK/Malaysia), acoustic stylings from the Hops (UK), DJ Crystof (Latvia), dub reggae sound systems, audio art from the sonic arts artist festival and much more . . . entry by donation!

Well Furnished Evicted!

Posted: August 26, in **Uncategorized.**

At 6am this morning (26/08/11) Well Furnished was broken into by about 20 High Court Bailiffs with dogs. They also had support from Police Officers. We were completely unprepared for this. We were told by the court that we had eviction dates for 7th and 24th September.

The bailiffs were not too bad and let us recover some of our stuff However at one point they forced two of the Well Furnished crew through the gate and physically assaulted both of them. The police were unconcerned about the physical harm inflicted on us by the bailiffs. This was despite the fact we put up no resistance and were polite and civil, as we believe we have been throughout our time at Well Furnished since the end of April.

We think it is a very sad state of affairs that the property agents Lamberts and St John Hackney Joint Charities Trust have decided to spend charity money on a very costly eviction process.

The Trust claim they don't have enough money to renovate their properties, are making their existing tenants responsible for repairs and increasing the rents by up to 300%.

Well Furnished is not the only empty property on Well St and Terrace Rd, half of the Trust's properties are empty. This is a blight on the street, damaging for existing tenants businesses and a gross injustice for the people of Hackney who are supposed to be benefiting from the income made by renting out properties.

You can find out more about this on the Save Well Street Market Website.

We have always wanted to use the empty properties, Well Furnished and This and That for the benefit for the community as a whole. From the outset we have reached out to our neighbours and many of them have welcomed us, recognising that we have worked tirelessly to make the empty space beautiful and a asset for the community.

We have always tried to contact Lamberts, The Church Trust, The Vicar and Geoff T (local councilor and chairman of the Trust), however they have never answered any of emails or phone calls.

If you liked what we were doing at Well Furnished and feel that Lamberts could have handled this differently, please let them know.

Please email

****

and/ or

****

Response to statement by bailiffs' on Well Furnished eviction

Posted: September 5, in **Uncategorized**

Edited on 5 September 2011:

We've just noticed that the sheriff's office have written their own article:

SQUATTER EVICTION IN HACKNEY

by ******** on 27 August 2011

On Friday, The Sheriffs Office cleared a large squat in Terrace Road, Hackney, East London removing twenty adult squatters from a shop and four flats.

Acting on behalf of our client, who was recently bequeathed the premises as part of a legacy, we used a Writ of Possession to gain High Court approval to enter the building, by force if necessary, and take possession of the property by evicting the squatters who had been illegally squatting for up to a year.

The premises were linked and had at one time been one large shop with living accommodation above in a parade of shops. Although the squatters had installed a CCTV system to warn them of possible eviction, the eviction team bypassed the cameras and surprised them in the early hours of the morning, clearing all of the properties simultaneously.

Supported by a police presence of eight officers, we had removed all but two of the squatters by 7:40 am. We also helped the squatters to remove all of their personal belongings. One female squatter tried to re-enter the premises and was restrained by a Police Officer while another refused to leave and had to be physically escorted from the premises. The premises were restored to their proper owners by 9 am that morning.

I'm delighted that the eviction went smoothly. The Police were supportive and, as usual, worked with our own enforcement officers in unison, assisting where necessary. Unlike other enforcement companies, The Sheriffs Office is very much in support of the proposed new laws to make squatting a criminal offence in England and Wales.

Source: http://www.thesheriffsoffice.com/articles/squatter_eviction_in_hackney/

Corrections:

— They did not remove *'twenty adult squatters'*, they removed 'only' 17 homeless people and kicked them out on to the street in the early hours of the morning, in the rain, the Friday before a bank holiday weekend when it would have been pretty much impossible to get support, advice and possibly temporary emergency housing from the appropriate agencies.

— As previously mentioned, it wasn't really necessary to obtain a Writ of Possession to gain High Court approval. We had been in fairly constant contact with the courts, finding out when the bailiffs were due to evict us. We had been occupying three properties, two shop units and the flats above, and we had been informed by the Court Service that the eviction for the shops was due on 7 September and the flats were due to be evicted on 24 September.

— It's surprising that someone who is writing an article for the Sheriffs Office including the text *'squatters who had been illegally squatting for up to a year'* apparently doesn't know the difference between illegal and unlawful. Squatting isn't illegal, it's not a crime, it's a civil wrong, a matter for the civil courts. We should have thought that the Sheriffs Office of all people ought to know the difference, since they're carrying out evictions as a result of such proceedings.

— The properties were not *'recently bequeathed the premises as part of a legacy'*, the properties have been owned by the trust for a considerable length of time and have been arguably mismanaged, certainly neglected and allowed to become seriously dilapidated. The background is well-known locally, in that the owners and their managing agents have been trying to force out other legitimate shop tenants through raising rents by as much as 300 per cent, many of the shops on the street have been vacated due to the owner's and their managing agent's unreasonable demands.

— *'The squatters had installed a CCTV system'* is also factually incorrect. Some of the squatters are artists, and video cameras had been re-sited as an art installation as a commentary about the surveillance society, as the UK is one of the most surveilled societies in the world. It is factually incorrect to suggest that the sheriffs 'eviction team' had somehow cleverly 'bypassed the cameras', which were not plugged in, and not connected to any monitors. In fact, it wasn't difficult at all for the sheriffs to gain entry, as one of the squatters had left early that morning to go to work and so the main door to the courtyard had not only been left unlocked and unbarricaded, it had been left open, so no force was required.

— *'We also helped the squatters to remove all of their personal belongings.'* Again, this is factually incorrect. The majority of the sheriffs were very obstructive and refused to let people collect their belongings. However, a couple of them were more reasonable and amenable, and helped one of the squatters, who has a disability and isn't able to carry heavy things. After we had all vacated the premises those individual sheriffs also went back into the building to retrieve some personal possessions including a bag containing someone's passport (Thanks guys, you know who you are, we appreciated your help!). We certainly were not permitted to remove all of our personal belongings. As things stand, we have made repeated phone calls to a number given on a notice affixed to the gate, yet no one has returned our calls to tell us when we can have our belongings back. At the moment, they are withholding many personal possessions, including documents, clothes, bedding, mattresses, all our pots and pans and cooking equipment from the kitchen. Most importantly, someone who wasn't living at Well Furnished, but was storing a bag there for safety (because we weren't due to be evicted till 7 and 24 September) has been repeatedly asking the 24/7 security guards to retrieve a bag containing her passport. This person is a European citizen and she can't go home or travel anywhere without her passport and it will be difficult for her to get a replacement while she's stuck in the UK. It is, basically, a lie to say that they helped the squatters remove all of their personal belongings when more than a week later they are still withholding someone's bag containing a passport and also lots of other personal effects belonging to many of us, given that we were rudely awakened in the early hours of the morning and evicted unexpectedly well before the date the Court Service told us we were due to be evicted.

— *'One female squatter tried to re-enter the premises and was restrained by a Police Officer . . .'* Again, this assertion is factually incorrect. One squatter did not try to re-enter the premises, she simply attempted to remove from the gate a padlock, which was the property of the squatters. As she removed the padlock and passed it to one of the other squatters, she was physically grabbed and assaulted by the sheriffs as the police stood by and let them. She has photographic evidence of bruising to her arm, which left marks in the shape of finger prints where she had been physically manhandled by the sheriffs, and her nose was also bashed. As mentioned above, we were all being polite and not-resisting, and yet suddenly without warning, they grabbed her from behind and assaulted her.

— *' . . . while another refused to leave and had to be physically escorted from the premises.'* This is misleading as well. What actually happened was that one squatter who had been staying in Well Furnished effectively had to remove not only her things, but those of the squatter who had left early that morning to go to work, and also some electrical goods belonging to someone else. The sheriffs originally said that if she left, someone else could come back into the building to help carry stuff out, but when she phoned the squatters who had already left the building to ask for help and to coordinate the changeover she was told that they were refusing to let anyone else back in. It took a considerable amount of time to try to pack her clothes and those of the person who was out at work, given that the eviction wasn't expected until 7 and 24 September. It wasn't possible for her to remove all those belongings without assistance. When she crossed the courtyard, she realised that just outside the gate were sheriffs with barking dogs straining at their leads. She was asked to leave the premises, but explained that she had an autistic spectrum disorder and, further, was afraid of dogs and wanted the dogs to be moved away. The sheriffs declined to move the dogs and started moving towards her and saying something about physically removing her from the premises. Again, we had been very polite and hadn't been resisting the eviction, and that person had clearly made her phobia about dogs known to the sheriffs who ignored her repeated pleas to remove the dogs. The dogs were not very well controlled, in fact they were particularly badly behaved as the dog handler was later witnessed yanking the dog back on its lead and shouting 'Korva!' (which we understand is a Polish swear word) at it. The squatter was terrified of the dogs and eventually a police officer came in through the gate and offered to help the squatter leave, promising to stay at all times between the dog and the squatter as she left the building. If the sheriffs had complied with the reasonable request to move the dogs round the corner away from someone who was visibly and audibly terrified of the dogs, who had notified them that she had an autistic spectrum disorder, then it would not have been necessary for the police officer to come to her assistance.

Well Evicted

Because I sincerely want to end all domination and exploitation and to begin opening the possibilities for creating a world where there are neither exploited or exploiters, slaves or masters, I choose to grasp all of my intelligence passionately, using every mental weapon — along with the physical ones — to attack the present social order. I make no apologies for this, nor will I cater to those who out of laziness or ideological conception of the intellectual limits of the exploited classes refuse to use their intelligence. It is not just a revolutionary anarchist project that is at stake in this struggle; it is my completeness as an individual and the fullness of life that I desire.

— Wolfi Landstreicher, *Against the Logic of Submission*

'Here lay the site of the well; the source of water and the heart of the community.'

— Graffiti inside the Well Furnished Social Centre

Bailiffs trampled back and forth over our banner that read HOUSING IS A HUMAN RIGHT, now laying in a puddle in front of the iron gates that had protected our yard.

As we gathered amongst the growing rain and watched the innumerable hi-visibility jackets struggling with their dogs, the upper windows of the flats connecting our block were flung open, and the crew of mild-mannered hipsters hung out the windows to gawp at the puddle of humanity in the streets below. Old Jo just happened at that point to come trundling past and spy them on the fourth floor. She took the opportunity to give a raucous but misinformed caterwaul.

'Why don't you lot get a job and pay rent like the rest of us?'

And they cheerfully replied:

'We do!'

We couldn't help but laugh bitterly into the drizzle. People looking like squatters, but the rent-gap a yawning chasm between us. It created a weird vignette against the early morning spit.

We couldn't really blame Old Jo for not supporting us — a local to the area she had dropped round numerous times to our social centre and given us vocal, relentless, East-End style support up until the moment she discovered the huge, gender-bending pornographic Graeco-Roman-style mural emblazoned across the bar we'd built. Even when we meekly tried to cover one of the more overt phalluses, penetrating an androgynous girl-boy, with a fire extinguisher she had not been placated. This was obviously still a bit raw with her, despite a resident hippy's claim to 'freedom of speech'. She'd been apoplectic to an almost comic degree, referring in a curmudgeonly way to how she had once 'been a hippy', but all-in-all the incident had harmed our relationships in the area.

Initially conceived at the invitation of local residents struggling under a 300% rent hike by the charitable trust that managed the properties 'for the benefit of the poor people of Hackney', as quoth by its centuries old charter. The boy scout centre, the Caribbean food store, a bakery, a toystore and bric-a-brac hub and the eponymous Well Furnished furniture store (ironically barren of kit until we refurbished it with the plentiful castaways found in nearby tower-block bins) all had lain empty for years as the trust seemingly worked to drive out the independent businesses and convert Well Street into yet another carbon-copy high street. Well Street was historically home to a thriving market, where Mr Cohen of subsequent Tesco fame (as legend has it) sold dented tins of paint to make his fortune. Now, it was another example of the power of a megamart in collusion with corrupt and oxymoronically named 'trusts' to gouge a hole in the heart of a community.

The Tesco looming in its central piazza, with its brew-crew of street people loitering outside, dominates the entire street, poignantly mirrored by the long-squatted house number 645 above the Laundromat, guarded by CCTV cameras, sucking the identity out of the local area. There is another Tesco, even bigger, not even ten minutes walk down Morning Lane. Our aim had been a show of solidarity with the tenants, occupying and re-energising dead spaces with workshops, performances, meet-and-greets for the variegated tribes that dwelled in Hackney. One night, I took a stroll through the expansive space, surveying our creation: in one room, a radical anthropology talk by the fabled Goldsmiths lecturer Chris Knight, discussing the role of women in pre-patriarchal society; next door, a circus skill workshop lead by the twelve-year old kid from next door, sharing his Diablo skills with a troupe of grungy itinerants; outside in the courtyard, several of the resident spoken word artists were having an impromptu jam, sharing their latest writing; and then through the kitchen to an area of steel poles where the spandex-clad 'pole athletics' group were flexing up to pounding samba-dance rhythms. A girl on roller-skates coasted serenely through the whole scene.

Our corner of Homerton was booming with performance poets at the time, and our poetry events beneath the 'source of the well' banner were verbal bacchanals full of spontaneity and feverish outbursts. It seemed like the whole crowd had something to contribute, audience and performers flowing from one to the other across that imaginary fourth wall, holding public conversations with whoever stepped into the spotlight we hung at one end of the room. At one of the genesis events, I met a furious poet with a signature fund-raising technique. To a braying crowd he proclaimed that for every ten beers sold at the bar he would remove an item of clothing onstage, culminating after forty beers with a burlesque to unpeel a velvet green doublet to the ullulating bass of 'Shake Your Rump'. It had gotten the crowd drinking, perhaps necessary self-medicating in some cases, and fed a narrative of wild abandon through the night of spoken word and feral theatre. The night had been eclectic, with the majority of the crowd performing onstage at some point, or in the least as guerilla hecklers and spontaneous rap battlists. In addition to the crusty striptease, Gothic pirates and nervous virgins had pouted and bombasted in warrior verse and smutty rhyme; a man dressed as a giant goblin had screeched poetry about urban knife-battles; a rapper with a lisp had recited a hip-hop version of *A Midsummer Night's Dream.*

The poet scuffled up behind the bar and began to drape a hip-hop motley of tattered clothes over his scarecrow frame. Catching his eye, I raised a supportive can of Red Stripe towards him.

'I'd never met a third sector sex worker before. It's like charity stripping.'

'Solidarity stripping mate, but this isn't a career, more a one time thing for the moment. All the money we raise tonight goes to a grassroots autonomous community out in the boondocks The irony being they're all in recovery from drug addiction. Cheers!'

He toasted my can and pulled deep on his own beer, winking over the ringpull.

'I gotta run mate, we're getting evicted in the morning and I'm supposed to be barricading. No rest for the wicked, eh?'

'I admire your dedication,' I conceded.

He laughed.

'Needs must, mate, needs must. When you are desperate, you do things you wouldn't normally.'

*

I'd been invited into the collective after meeting Felicity at a spoken word show under a railway arch in Waterloo, where she'd performed a piece on squatting which grabbed my interest. Felicity had a heart of pure gold, and the energy of a whirling dervish. In the time we lived together, she set up the gardens, filling old boots and tin cans with the ripe horse manure Doc Homerton brought from a freecycle donor. She coordinated with all the neighbours, almost daily doing the rounds to speak to the concerned local tenants who had a streak of solidarity with the squatters in the area due to a mutual threat of eviction. She ran the gauntlet of being a central hub of our unit, whilst simultaneously undergoing the media training for the SQUASH campaign and performing live several times a week. Together, we'd commenced rallying a challenge to the trust's management of the properties, preparing questions for the Charity Commission on the aims and objectives of such an organisation. We found the chairman of the charity also sat on a property management group's board with a vested interest in the neighbourhood of Well Street, highlighted as it was for 'urban renewal'. Essentially newspeak for gentrification, the whole area had been marked for replacement with high rent paying chain stores and coffee houses.

A long early debate focused on the use of the word 'alternative', concerned members highlighting how that word had been appropriated to mask the sinister intent of arts projects as the vanguard of gentrification. We earnestly discussed the tyranny of 'we', the assumption of solidarity in danger of becoming a yoke of slavery around the dispossessed's neck. In seeking to identify and understand ourselves, we turned to Dutch sociologist Hans Pruijt, who separates squatters into five distinct categories of need:

1. Deprivation based
    — i.e. homeless people squatting for housing need.
2. An alternative housing strategy
    — e.g. people unprepared to wait on municipal lists to be housed taking direct action.
3. Entrepreneurial — e.g. people breaking buildings to service the need of a community for cheap bars, clubs etc.
4. Conservational — i.e. preserving monuments because the authorities have let them decay.
5. Political — e.g. activists squatting buildings as protests or to make social centres.

Most significantly for me, above the sink in the little kitchen compartment of the furniture store, someone had scrawled:

THE DEFINITION OF SQUATTING AND OCCUPATION

1) SQUATTING — sitting around and leaving a bit of shit behind.
2) OCCUPATION — a full-time job.

Yet within a social centre such as Well Furnished, these divisions became very blurred. As a collective, we fulfilled all of the above criteria, and often found that one fed directly into the other.

Those in need — homeless people — founding an alternative housing strategy in order to generate income, provide services for the local and extended community, whilst simultaneously conserving a decaying property and practicing our political ideals. Indeed, the politicisation of our actions, the overarching drive of anarchy, meant that the preceding four criteria were an essential foundation for the final.

Often, we joked about it being a full-time occupation, yet one that constantly battled against repression from within and without. The neighbours on Valentine Road hated us with such vehemence that they threw water over the wall to soak a small acoustic party that had formed in the courtyard. They organised themselves into the Valentine Action Group — delightfully acronymed to VAG — and sent leaflets to all the neighbours asking: 'what should we do about the squatters?' At the same time we were attending the local Well Street Trader's meetings, trying to find our way into sympathetic local relations.

The community poetry event advertised on the website failed to materialise as the organiser — myself — was too hungover and broken to get off the leather sofa next to the shopfront window to organise it. It was not the first time good intentions succumbed to my addictions.

My actions, my recklessness at that time, often triggered such incidents. Upon finding a trapdoor to the rooftops four storeys above Well Street, I sat up on the apex with a beer in the sunshine, saluting the occupiers in the courtyard below. The VAG called the police and a crew of them tricked someone into opening the gate and they swarmed in, giving it their best 'naughty-and-nice' police routine. We gave them some names and they left, having found that we obviously were not 'breaking in with power tools' as the VAG had reported.

An eviction becomes a shattering thing to such ambitions — your basic needs swell up and quash the lofty aspirations that grow in a shelter of relative comfort. The eviction came as a severe shock as two weeks before we successfully resisted an attempt on 'Lithuania' — the two-up/two-down gatehouse that protected the access to the courtyard. Named after the loveable East European kids who occupied it, living cheek-by-jowl and still sharing their bath and shower with the dozen or so grubby do-gooders in the furniture shop next door. The lock-up on Lithuania was superlative — heavy bike locks and a steel door over the front access. Our victory had been in the battle, but was to cost us heavily when they returned unannounced two weeks later to drive us out.

Businesslike and proper, some members of the collective managed to address the representatives of bureaucracy and examine their paperwork as the men with battering rams ran around the building, looking for doors to smash down. It would take years before one member of the collective would inform me retrospectively that it was, of course, totally illegal what they did. At the time, they argued that all of the properties were already covered by a High Court order, making it a criminal offence to be in occupation of any of them. The bailiffs were able to enact the eviction even though the official date had been given as somewhere in October. As one property backed on to another, they were able to sweep through unchecked.

A person's attitude in the face of humiliating, brutal and shocking defeat is character defining. As the rain fell, we shared out rain jackets and covered our possessions with what tarps and plastic we had. Someone bought and distributed hot milky coffee laced with sugar. Friends arrived with bikes and trailers, and we arranged to transport everyone and everything to a squat in Victoria Park — less than two kilometres away.

645

We will ask nothing, we will demand nothing, we will take. OCCUPY.

— Graffiti on Hackney Road, 2012

Anarchy is good for you.

— Graffiti on 645 wall

Four days later we took the property directly opposite Well Furnished, still owned by the charitable trust: a three-storey corner terrace building over a laundromat, looking out over the Tesco.

From the kitchen windows of 645, we looked over at Well Furnished, waving cheerily at the security guards who lingered around the iron gates, begging cherry tomatoes from the yard and trying to wangle back our various possessions still locked inside. 645 was much more stereotypically 'squatty': the insides were a web of graffiti and scrawled slogans. The various rooms were filled with the detritus of previous occupants: one room full of used syringes, another holding a gay porn DVD, mask and homemade spanking device. We even found two wraps of double dropped sugar cubes inside a cereal packet, left as a little sweetener for the next occupiers.

When we lived over the road in the ostensibly 'drug-free' social centre, 645 had been like a one-stop narcotics shop. You could pop round anytime day or night and go door-to-door asking what people had for sale. One night we took a lot of speed and stayed up playing a frenzied game of Pictionary. Another time we scored a load of ketamine before heading out to the Sextek party in Vauxhall — a filthy, debased night of hard techno and industrial with dark rooms, glory holes, and a seedy mix of squat debauchery.

Whilst living at 645, we investigated the other empty properties on that row of houses, climbing up on to the roof and counting the buildings until we came to one that was empty. Some friends of ours needed housing, so we took them up and over to one terrace that was, according to sources in the neighbourhood, empty. Cracking the roof hatch, we lowered ourselves down into the house, finding it unnervingly fully furnished. There were clothes drying on the hanger, and outside one door, a pair of trainers. Creeping in, I peered into the room, and inside the bed could make out the shape of someone peacefully slumbering.

I froze, considering bundling them up and throwing them out the door. It could have been a security guard, an anti-squatter, or even a legitimate resident. Either way, this house was taken, so I gave a silent signal to the others climbing in behind me, and we fled back to 645.

It wasn't all fun and games. One night I came back to find the house in uproar, everywhere tense, panicked faces, suddenly fearful of one another. Someone had been through the communal laptop, which had been shared very publicly and liberally at Well Furnished, and found in the hard drive a cache of pornography: the kind of pornography that ruins lives and shatters reputations, the kind of pornography that lands people in jail with the irremovable label of 'pervert'.

The atmosphere was horrendous. A veritable witch hunt, with everyone a suspect, was possible. This had the power to totally destroy what we had created together, all our mutual trust and collectivism. It was only by the chance discovery of one clue that a member of our group was able to identify who had downloaded the images. I decided to test that hunch, and when he came home, I met him at the door.

'We found the pictures,' was all I said.

The look of realisation on his face confirmed every suspicion. He visibly crumbled.

Once people knew, reactions were mixed. Some people wanted to kill him, such was their disgust. Others agreed with him that it was a disease, and wanted to help him get help. We secluded him in a room upstairs, left him to meditate on the Medicine Buddha from Clifton Mansions whilst we debated what to do. Some people in the collective were near hysterical with outrage. Others discussed, in terms of harm, what had he actually done? Most compelling was the argument that regardless of your personal criticism of his actions, he had put us all at risk by putting the pictures on a communal laptop, and that the owner was the one at most risk of harm.

'Why not call the police?'

'The laptop isn't even his. It was communal. We'd all be under suspicion.'

'Can you imagine the headlines? "The Paedosquatters of Homerton".'

'We're not calling the filth. We have to solve our own problems.'

'It's a sickness. He said it himself, he's got the problem, not us.'

'We should try to help him.'

'He'll get plenty of help in a prison cell, the disgusting

pervert.'

'That is not helpful. We can refer him to some support services.'

'How is that solving our own problems? We should just kick the shit out of him — '

'Again, not helping. Violence is not a solution.'

'Of course it's a solution. The police use it all the time —'

'We are not the police, nor do we want to be.'

'Who are we to judge? Who has he actually harmed?'

'He's put the whole collective at risk.'

We let him sleep, and the next day, moved him out of the squat to a friend's place in Victoria Park. There he could hold up whilst he decided his next move. It was clear that he could no longer stay with us. Nobody could forget, even those who tried to help him. Eventually, word got out to Victoria Park too, and he had to leave the scene all together. It was a tragedy unfolding.

Perhaps the most sympathetic solution would have been to keep him with us, to help him however we could, to acknowledge that his problem was our problem, and that we should try and build structures of support and rehabilitation amongst ourselves to counter unacceptable deviance within our own community. In terms of creating a model of a future society in our present, we were given a perfect dilemma, a chance to practice what we preached, yet when it came to the crunch our collective actions lead to his banishment from the group. On balance, him choosing to remove himself from our circle was the easiest solution for us, and perhaps the shrewdest for him, considering the division in attitudes over what he had done. His continued presence could only have resulted in further fractiousness over him remaining a member of our group and in unavoidable conflict. As anti-authoritarians, we could, with clear conscience, neither shop him to the police or forcibly remove him, yet as ethical human beings neither could we condone or ignore the exploitation of minors, or that he had jeopardised the safety of everyone he lived with. He lost his friends, his home, his reputation. His name is no longer spoken amongst those who know what he has done. Exile and disgrace from his community seem like a far worse punishment than anything the State could deliver upon him. I hope the experience made him address the choices he was making in his life and enable him to change them. But of course, since he has gone, we have no way of knowing.

*

645's top floor had no doors. At night we lay in our separate sections listening to various arrangements of people making love, having sex, and balls out fucking in the rooms around us. Every day seemed to bring some new hook-up, a consequence of cramming nearly twenty people into a much smaller space than they had occupied before. Also, the drugs ban of Well Furnished had been relinquished, so me and my fellow indulgers were enjoying a heady blend of cocaine and MDMA that turned us into manic, babbling, loving machines.

In defiance of our eviction from the social centre, we went through a performance session right there in the front room of 645, hanging curtains over one side to make a stage, the mighty HOUSING IS A HUMAN RIGHT banner returning as a backdrop. All the faces who used to drop in at Well Furnished came, and we performed long into the night — poetry, music and hip-hop bellydancing mingling with the waves of laughter and joy soaking through the crowd. Yes, we'd been evicted, but that was nothing new, more like a change in the season than a catastrophic event.

Performing that night, I recited my piece about the Sextek party I visited months before, preambled as a letter written home to my parents:

Dear Mum and Dad:
Late one night stroll down SE1
Down an alleyway past the Vauxhall Tavern
Duck inside with pride, what do we find?
SEXTEK party — raging full grind
Yes they got the pounding, pounding techno music
Pounding, pounding techno music

Pounding techno, pounding techno
Pounding, pounding techno music
But — where's the sex?
Where's the sex? We got the tek, but where's the sex?
We got the tek, but where's the sex?
Two hundred confused people mope
Under the bridge in a grotty neon k-hole
We were promised dark rooms, fetish and glory holes!
Where's the wild fucking, the public playing, the fun?
Then — my ears twitch as I overhear them.

WONKY GERMAN ACCENT: *I've been here two hours and there's nothing happening.*

SPANISH: *You are part of the problem, man, you came to e-see a freakshow but you don't want to get involved.*

I am suddenly resolved!
Striving to be highly evolved, feeling terribly bold
I gird my loins and stroll
The bar — upstairs — I spot them:

One blonde, one brunette, PVC and fishnets,
Red lipstick and corsets
Leaning on the bar their boobs bursting bombastically from

basques as the techno bang, bang, bangs
That's them.
I approach the blonde
She turns an aquiline pout towards me,
Shadowed eyes steely dancing with glee
And I sputter the words, anticipation making my throat tight
'Are you looking for a slave for the night?'
She smiles, teeth like a tigress, and with an accent I found
exciting I must confess
She says: 'Que?'

She turns to her friend, a curvaceous black-haired lady of
torment,
A brief exchange, as they speak Spanish, and they figure out
what I meant
The black-haired one smiles, and turns to me with a grin
'My name is Mistress Rosa, let us begin.'

They approach and pin me, hands squeezing my throat
They hand me their bag, they hand me they coat
For the rest of the night, I carried whatever Mistress Rosa gave
For she was my Mistress, I was her slave.

(And in my best impression of her Spanish tones:)

'Tonight, for a while, we shall play a game
And when it is finished, everything shall return to the same,
We shall play with power, with pain, with fear,
And then afterwards we shall relax with a beer.'

'The code words are green, amber and red,
Remember them well, keep them in your head,
Green for go, amber warning, cry red to stop
Now get on your knees, and hand me my riding crop!'

Thwack! Whack! Crack! Slap! Punch! Pinch! Moan!
Thwack! Whack! Crack! Slap! Punch! Pinch! Groan!
They choke me till I nearly black out!
They kick me until I scream out!
They walk away and ignore me, I have to follow them about
They feed me drugs from their body parts,
They forever enchain my heart.

'Who is the greatest Mistress in the world?'
I roared: 'MISTRESS ROSA!'
'Who is the best mistress?'
The crowd roared: 'MISTRESS ROSA!'

Maybe in your eyes it is wrong, or a sin,
That from her creamy buttocks I snorted ketamine

Or watched from the corner of the dark room place
As she squatted and laughed and pissed in a stranger's face
And how did I feel as he emerged, gasping and refreshed
Ecstatic, erotic, by her urine blessed,
My mistress turned to me, and I knew what she said was true:
'You see that guy there? He's a better slave than you.'

Oh the shame! Oh the ignominy! To be second best slave!
Oh how my cheeks burned as I licked her latex boot at that rave
As she choked me, and poked me, and bit me and slapped
As we laughed and danced and did drugs and relaxed
Free from judgment, free from restraint, free from guilt
This is for what our human rights were built.

At the end of our play, we hugged and said fond farewells
Stepped out into the dawn and the Sunday morning church bells
Revived from a night where we played with consent
Without fear
Where there is no harm to be strange,
Where it is no crime to be queer
So come out of your dungeons, your cupboards, your closets
Wearing your finest rubber bodysuits and latex Nun's habits
Join us in a world where we are open and no longer just poseurs
Who is the greatest Mistress in the world? It must be —

Everyone in the room screamed: 'MISTRESS ROSA!'

'Having a lovely time in London, your loving son, George.'

*

When eviction day rolled around, we were prepared. After the last eviction and the change in the law to criminalise squatting in residential properties looming, we rallied the local squatters and prepared to give a real show.

A tiny tea tent was set up in front of the Sitex door — tarp and a table laden with boiling water, biscuits and wafers — to both provide the troops with sustenance and create an effectively hazardous barrier for the bailiffs to cross. The HOUSING IS A HUMAN RIGHT banner flapped from the upstairs windows, and a sound system on a trailer bike blared suitably rebellious songs as people assembled to greet the forces of darkness. Thirty, then forty, then fifty people, an assorted rag-tag peasant's mob, gathered outside on their bikes and in their boots to sip tea and swap anecdotes.

The bailiffs arrived in their little van, and wandered hesitantly up to the masses to enquire politely as to who was in charge. Cheeky grins and quips rained back.

'Well, you guys know we'll be back.'

The two bailiffs were around less than ten minutes in all,

taking one look at the assembled peons and deciding against it. As they pulled away, a cheer erupted from the group.

But they weren't done — over on Mare Street another squat was awaiting bailiffs to visit. Our army joyously marched over to reassemble there, the bikers arriving quicker than others, but the main force marching proudly behind a huge red and black banner reading, RESIST EVICTIONS.

We paraded down Morning Lane, to scare off another pair of shocked looking bailiffs who had been sniffing around the second property. Smiles all round and that feeling of solidarity with other struggling strangers, old faces and new, neighbours and squatters from the other boroughs assembled by text-bombs and word of mouth. The second cheer of the morning went up as their van roared off.

We marched on, this time to the Tesco carpark to blockade shoppers from entering. Here, a small party broke out, a little miniature carnival of resistance as people broke out beers and jigged merrily to the music from the bike-boom-box.

I'd been to successful resistances before, organising early in the morning with other bleary-eyed squatters, always happy to visit another site and meet people in a similar situation. Often, with the first eviction attempt, only two or three bailiffs are in attendance, and the sight of a platoon of crusties awaiting them is enough to give them cause to think twice. Sometimes, if the occupiers are a bit green, they'll get inside before the troops are rallied. Other times they call the police and hang about a bit, before the police arrive and tell them there is nothing they can do. But this was this first resistance parade I'd encountered.

It's all in the knowledge of the essential futility. Squatters never win. Or at least, the victories are short lived. In the end, the forces of authority will return again and again to enforce the sacred rights of contract, ownership of property and the rule of law.

This is the point of resistance — not to win, but to drag your heels until the day that any victory for the opposition is purely Pyrrhic. To resist every eviction, every injustice, every instance of people being removed from shelter to be thrown out on the street.

Worldwide, it is estimated one in seven people are technically squatters — resident on land they have no legal claim to. The squatters of Europe and beyond stand in solidarity with a movement that is older than the system thrown up in the last few centuries to further oppress and exploit the people on the land. To resist, to refuse, to rebuke, to revolt and to rebel. To proudly be the scum of the nation, vilified by the state-sponsored press, harangued in the street by strangers and generally reviled by those whose security is threatened by the decisions we make and the choices we live.

I looked at those faces on that cold December morning, dancing around the Tesco car park, being gawped at by passersby and I realised that with comrades, with friends, with this squat-family, I would never go hungry, always have a place to crash, never suffer the fate of millions to be crushed by a system I was born, unchoosing, into. Together, we could hang, dangle-dancing on the end of society's rope, and carve out a little sanity in a mad world.

The Pigeon Coup

Smash down my door, six in the morning come the law
To protect me from myself and my wicked ways
And relieve me of my draw

— Inner Terrestrials, 'Law Dealers'

ALL BAILIFFS ARE CLASS TRAITORS.

I'd been overseas, visiting the autonomen housing projects in Berlin and the kraaks of Amsterdam. When I arrived back to the Pigeon Coup, I was there only twelve hours before we were evicted into the grey streets of London Fields.

We were all awake in the front room, sharing rollies and cups of bitter tea, when the sound of an angle grinder broke the silence and the doors below were heaved asunder.

The night before, we'd talked before of sluicing the concrete stairwell with Fairy Liquid — something there was an abundance of in the house due to the number of professional bubblers living there — or mounting faux-signs at the door warning of armed responses and attack dogs. We'd mooted greasing ourselves up and wrestling with bailiffs through the floors, of rolling barrels downstairs as people entered, of a hundred-and-one responses to another eviction. Our meagre response upon being awoken hungover and disbelieving was to stack assorted clutter and shite behind the doors — which opened outwards anyway.

The now familiar wake up of 'Police! Police!' shouted through the house, the gut-wrenching realisation that it was happening *again*, scanning faces for anything other than resignation and despondency, angst and confusion. The crushing inevitability of it all swings into effect, and the only response is to sit and drink tea beneath the slogan, ALL BAILIFFS ARE CLASS TRAITORS.

WPC Jennings was first into the kitchen.

'Alright everyone, if we could just get you to collect your belongings and make your way out, that would be jolly nice! We are human beings too.'

She was young. Probably not even a couple of years on the force. Not fully rotten. I speculated that she was possibly handpicked for this assignment to help her develop a thicker skin.

She was certainly being presented with a pretty pitiful sight. A lounge full of miscreant crusties and weirdos, not activists, radicals, art students or even East Europeans, just the dregs of the unsheltered, those desperate enough to occupy a building known to be awaiting its second eviction attempt. Chancers.

The bailiffs were milling around, studiously ignoring the criticism blazed in six foot high letters on the bricks behind them. Two more police were inside. We began, what we now knew, would be quite a leisurely unpacking of the house. The cupboards were cleared, the pots and pans, the mattresses, blankets, electrical appliances, tools slipped surreptitiously through chains of people, watching to see if anyone objected. Then as we got bolder; the crowbars went out, the massive bolt croppers, and finally a six metre ladder was slid down one window and collected from the street. We moved on to the kitchen utensils, and ultimately the freezer, which contained one frozen dead crow in a plastic ziplock bag. One of the residents had an amateur interest in taxidermy, and had been saving it whilst they located the sawdust.

Upstairs, a Czech with no English but a recently littered Staff terrier was absorbing the attention of the police, one of whom was bitten by the dog as she entered the room, having ignored the warning biroed on the door. The other police shrugged it off, and she sullenly waited outside whilst they tried to negotiate. We giggled to each other in the corridors, whispering 'good dog'.

The police called up a special number to a Czech translator, and communicated with the dog's owner through the disembodied voice on their phone. The dog was temporarily taken into care in Battersea, the puppies vaccinated and fostered, and the mother returned.

The accumulated furnishings, bags and trolleys filled the pavement outside, where the world was waking up. Passerbys screwed their heads round as they cantered past to catch the bus, local kids hanging around gawping, little screwfaces boggling at the reality before them. These kids from the local estate, who stole phones to sell, had access to crack cocaine if you needed, whose elder cousins slipped into our parties to huff nitrous oxide from balloons and stare incredulously as we cavorted wildly in front of speakers too big for the room. Later, they would be stealing stuff and attacking the stragglers right there on the pavement.

There was no organisation this time. I had dropped back in on my way from Amsterdam to see who was still occupying, finding a house full of hostile strangers and old squat neighbours from the darker side of the crease. Even in Amsterdam, where we had hitchhiked from Berlin to catch a budget bus over the water, the tiny two room flat we had been hosted in had been awaiting eviction. Sometimes it seemed like everywhere we went was on that list. The Dutch squatters — *kraakers* — were militant, highly organised, still fighting back despite the criminalisation of squatting. The red, black and green ant logo was everywhere in their neighbourhood — the symbol of the Peoples' Army — and they showed us videos of their opening style. They would go in the middle of the day, in a large group, and cover the door with a sheet whilst three people went inside with tools. A quirk of the law in Holland means that in order to be classed as a squat, the building needs to have a bed, a table and chair. So, these were duly delivered from around the corner once the door was open. The kraakers all had a piece of black Lego tattooed on their wrist — a wry joke about the Black Bloc. They were all really into permaculture, and we sat up nights smoking outrageously good hashish smuggled from Morocco, talking about the different functions of plants and trees, dreaming of finding gardens one day where we could be out of this madness.

The curse of freedom — those who live in these grey areas, soft places, between the cracks of society — succumbing to the lull of liberty's sweet sonata, aspirations of indomitability crumbling into indulgence and the immediacy of satiety.

When presented with the forces of darkness, as they are affectionately known, in a setting such as the Pigeon Coup, it is important to still remember that they too are oppressed, and acting in the manner of oppressed people everywhere, by exercising their limited acquisition of power to keep themselves one level above those below; the nature of hierarchy. WPC Jennings, the other officers, and the bailiffs too were, undeniably, human beings operating within a system that dehumanises both themselves and those around them.

So yet another home was abandoned to sit empty, awaiting the next set of squatters to reopen it. It happened before, and doubtless would happen again. Such is the process of resistance, of self-actualisation, and indeed, of squatting.

Having visited the 'squats' (actually housing projects with licence) of Berlin, I can vouch for the benefits of a good, regular eviction. Transformation and change are often hard, but necessary for growth and development in a positive sense, despite the hassle. As the legislative system turns its beady eye back to the misnomer that is 'squatter's rights', I am resolute in the knowledge that whatever is said, squatting will stay. It's necessity and practicality guarantee that the oldest form of land tenure in the world will continue to evolve and provide shelter for the needy, regardless of its legal status.

As we were escorted from the premises, the locksmiths were already taking off ours and putting on theirs. I thought about the time I lived there, wondered why it always seemed to start raining when we were evicted. This was the building that had the weird stencil on the toilet door, of a man escaping through barbed wire, a building previously squatted by Tanya, before I met her, and by many others. We laughed and played there, blowing bubbles out the window when the bailiffs first came to evict, a wall of people singing songs and glaring from masks as the authorities tried to muscle through.

But, still: ALL BAILIFFS ARE CLASS TRAITORS.

Welcome to Fortress Hampstead

The cause of homelessness is lack of housing.

— Jonathan Kozol

Many people without secure housing and the comforts of a stable home have been to the mansion mausoleum of The Bishops Avenue in Hampstead.

In a low-budget tribute to the housing porn available via mainstream media and the high street frontage of estate agent's shops (in full view of both children and the homeless, I might add), my friends and I used to wander through the absentee millionaire's row at curious hours of the morning. We would goggle incredulously through iron bars and wire mesh fencing at the decaying ruins and garden-forests.

They looked like the kind of places you'd choose to occupy and defend during a zombie apocalypse, places where a community could sow their crops, raise their kin and live a peaceful life, undisturbed by the violent cannibal insanity outside of their walls. How many families could live in such spaces, if they had to out of necessity? Some rooms within could surely take two or even three traditional sized families, even those infected with the virus. We hypothesised where the vegetable plots could be dug in, the children's playground erected, the trailer park levelled, and which places for the machine gun nests to fight off wandering zombie herds.

No lights glowed in the cavernous hulks shipwrecked in the doldrums of the heath, only the slow motion creak of disrepair. The waste of it all brought moments of mania, and in a frenzy we'd attempt to climb in, to begin to bring the space back to life, but our saner friends held us back and cried not to even try, not to even dare. We had heard the tales of what happened to those who snapped before.

Police helicopters had been the first warning sign when associates of ours attempted to occupy one building in the area. Searchlights hit the windows of the vast mansion they had found access to, joined shortly by the sound of guard dogs in the garden, and sirens in the distance.

Insecure, they fled in terror at the ferocity of the action taken against them. Abandoning the mansion, they dodged their pursuers and escaped into the streets, but to no avail. They were found hiding under a car parked in a nearby street and arrested on burglary charges.

In fear for our liberty, we were forced into leaving the great resources of The Bishops Avenue to urban foxes and security guards. As with the focus remaining on near-mythical benefits fraud rather than endemic tax evasion, the rich will be allowed to leave mansions empty whilst the government whines about under-occupancy in two bedroom council housing.

I'd been to West Hampstead only twice before. The first time, in August 2011, was in solidarity with a call-out made by a crew who found themselves besieged by a tat-thirsty mob of media. The scandal was the alleged displacement of occupiers caused when a dozen people entered a residential building to find shelter. The accusers — a wealthy doctor and his pregnant wife. It was the *coup d'etat* in a year long campaign of slander and misrepresentation under the general premise of scaring people into thinking their house could be squatted if they popped out to buy some muesli or some bags of pre-sliced frozen vegetables.

Grabbing our banner and spontaneously donning suits, we rode through the empty twilight suburbs to offer solidarity and, if necessary, get our media line out to the press. The people we met when we arrived were visibly shaken by the hostility directed at them, vulnerable but relieved to see some supportive faces. The media had already dispersed when we arrived around midnight, but the residents relived their experience with the flashback clarity of post-trauma distress.

'There was a pack of them, all cameras and questions, and they wanted a comment. I spoke to them. I wish I bloody hadn't. They went right for me. I told them we didn't mean to displace anyone, that we are cleaning the place and we'll move on. That we're really, really sorry.'

The dozen people all shared the sentiment, the remorse and horror evident in their expressions as they moved around the labyrinthine suburban terrace meekly gathering their clothes and brushing dust into pans. The image they cut would compete in heart jerking empathy with any photo of a doctor and his pregnant wife looking put out at having to stay another night or two in their apartment. But the media was pointedly blinkered in portraying that view of the story.

We hovered around, chatting amicably over tea and being as polite as possible, but the stress had obviously frayed them to the brink of shattering. One guy was into the Special Brew, and his polite front began to demonstrably erode after half an hour.

He pointed his frustrations point blank at us like the barrel of a beer flavoured gun.

'You bloody guys, frigging squat action heroes coming over here with your banner and your suit . . . '

Taking the hint but not the offence, we said our thanks and gave them our number in case they needed any more support. A few weeks later, we took the Special Brew guy in when they fled to the relative calm of Hackney, on condition that he kept his drinking and aggression under control, and let him sleep in our front room with his mate.

My second visit was nine months later, when I visited a comrade in Hampstead who was had a deal with the owner. A tall, bizarrely tiered terrace which had housed dozens of people, they had been invited in when the previous occupants were evicted by the landlord. He even passed them a key, and was happy for them to stay there and use the space. It hummed with the smell of black bean and smoked sausage stew, and we sucked Red Stripe reminiscing about the bad old days when we'd been customer liaisons, formerly known as 'teachers', at a language school in Waterloo.

That visit involved a banner as well, a good four metre grey tarp that we spent the evening painting. In giant black lettering read the rather awkward slogan of YOUR EVICTION IS MY EVICTION.

*

So-called 'squatter's rights' were created primarily to protect the rights of tenants facing illegal evictions by unscrupulous landlords. In the 1990s, the Conservative party mobilised to remove these rights, and was roundly defeated by the concerted actions of SQUASH — the Squatters Action for Secure Homes. In 2011, caught unawares by a rushed through tag-on to the Legal Aid and Social Policing Bill, squatting in residential properties became a criminal offence. Despite being roundly condemned by the Metropolitan Police and charities such as Shelter, in September of that year a boy named Alex Haigh became the first person to be sentenced and convicted for squatting. At the time of writing, a challenge to Section 144 is awaiting a court date which may result in a repeal of the law.

The Place to Be

When I arrived at the Place, the people in the basement were screaming.

A crew of half-naked people were wailing and bellowing at each other in the vast pillared basement of the Place. One naked girl was strapped to a textile cog, a man in a rubber gasmask trailing a cat o'nine over her supine body. Around them, a whirlwind of flesh and pain, gibbering and shrieking at each other.

'They're rehearsing a play. It's a BDSM version of *Faust*.'

I laughed with relief, and we were escorted upwards to the higher floors.

The Place seemed perfect. A three storey behemoth snuggled away in the back passages of Kentish Town, formerly a production house. There were kitchens on all the floors, and the upper two had individual offices with glass sliding doors built into them, perfect for individual squatters to nest in. From an opening crew of eight the summer before, friends had invited friends until the official occupancy rate varied between 20 and 30. Its size meant that it could easily take in evicted groups of refugee squatters from the area as the rolling waves of evictions moved through the city. They even managed to squeeze a music rehearsal room into the ground floor. There were regular theatrical rehearsals in the ample basement.

The kitchen divisions and the different floors meant that it was easy to live there without being disturbed by others. The uppermost was occupied by the original openers, people I'd known and loved since Well Street back in Hackney. These were the 'professional squatters', dedicated organisers, veterans and activists who experienced squatting idealistically, as much more than free rent, as a statement of intent, a declaration of rebellion and rejection of normality. Osmond was living there, looking fresh and positive, his days dedicated to his arts.

'All theory is grey, my friend. But forever green is the tree of life,' he'd laugh, collecting the one pound a week we all paid in so we could collectively buy toilet paper, teabags and sugar to share.

The middle floor had been occupied by a group who, due to

their dominant nationailty, were lazily referred to as 'the Lithuanians' — Polish music students, Hungarian biologists, Latvian baristas and Romanian bike-fixers. Economic migrants, working to improve their lives and their situations. They had been around for a while, most of them, and some carried a reputation for parasitism — they didn't skip so much food, they didn't clean up, a few of them had nationalism and chauvinism following them around like a bad smell. But they smiled, and told jokes, and were nice people and happy to boot.

'Everything transitory is but an image,' Osmond said as he emptied the bins, stomping on can after can after can after can of beer for the recycling. 'If you treat an individual as he is, he will remain how he is. But if you treat him as if he were what he ought to be and could be, he will become what he ought to be and could be.'

Whereas the upper floors had barred glass windows through which natural light could slink in, the bottom floor was a cave. The basement of the Place frequently hosted relentless high BPM drugfests of white powder indulgence that could spill on for days in a frenzy of stimulants and alcohol. At times, you could wander through and find wild-eyed maniacs snorting cocaine off of juggling knives whilst people wiggled and danced and shrieked at one another.

'Whatever you can do or dream you can, begin it. Boldness has genius, power and magic in it!' said Osmond, balancing a knife on the tip of one finger, his top hat at a rakish angle.

I was given an upper room. The place already had bailiffs booked on it when I arrived, but they weren't due for another month, and as they were county court, people were confident we could retain the Place. I had to find hobbies. Without the imminent threat of homelessness, I found myself with a new terror — that of not just occupying a building, but occupying myself.

'As soon as you trust yourself, you will know how to live,' said Osmond, winking conspiratorially as he broomed the top floor clear for the rehearsals to begin.

Secure in the Place to Be, I got into it.

I wrote a play about squatters for Osmond, set in a time when all squatting is illegal, when the streets were filled with food riots, where the police broke in with guns not paperwork. We wanted to put it on in abandoned buildings, to show the scenes of our lives from skipping, to barricading, to the court rooms. Osmond and I brainstormed ideas and I wrote as much as I could in my little editing suite, feeling like a poet in a garret, listening to Rachmaninov and smoking smuggled tobacco from

Lithuania, Germany and Catalunya.

'The greatest thing in this world is not so much where we stand as in what direction we are moving.'

We rode out to resistances in the area, arguing with police outside as the inhabitants were evicted into the street. We sheltered evicted crews in our downstairs room. I made thick, black, homebrew stout in old containers at the foot of my bed and we drank it lustily, tasting in it a whole dimension of difference from the mass produced Polish cans that were scarring our livers. We skipped chili plants out of the bin and kept them on the window sills, growing in the weak winter sunlight alongside trays of cress and pulses sprouting on cotton wool.

'I love those who yearn for the impossible.'

I wrote lurid, detailed erotica to an absent lover in the style of Anaïs Nin. I had an affair with a woman from another squat that ended in disaster, heartbreak and alienation. It felt like a normal, real life. People moaned about one another not cleaning, not doing the washing up, not skipping food. We sat up late talking impossible politics, drinking tequila, playing poker for pennies. I cooked huge vats of soup everyday and shared it with whoever was hungry — leek and potato, carrot and onion —

thick, nourishing, hippy slop that put a smile on the faces of people sick of eating sandwiches out of bins.

The week before the bailiffs were due, we began barricading. The windows were huge. There were four exits, but we got to work, feeling the jagged chains of stress in my gut grow tighter each day as the time drew nearer. The Lithuanians and Polish were talented, perfectionist carpenters, naturals with power tools and precise in their calculations. They explained how it was all pressure points, pure physics. Me and mine were more traditional, piling wood and metal and whatever crap we could find against the windows and bracing layer after layer against them. They looked terrible, but it was just a matter of style. We tried not to argue too much about it.

'If you've never eaten while crying you don't know what life tastes like,' said Osmond, looking disappointed at the piece of metal he'd ineffectually screwed over the fire exit.

*

The first people arrived around 8am. We greeted them with the first banner drop.

SQUATTERS RIGHTS OR SQUATTER RIOTS! hung from the massive front of the Place, brazen and uncompromising. Duval had quibbled about it, saying he didn't like it. I respected him for the barricade he built on one fire door — three days of making it impenetrable — but I'd also learned that he should be roundly ignored most of the time.

EAT THE RICH!

We hung on the windows in black masks as a crowd gathered below us. Friends from nearby squats, friends from as far back as Well Furnished, some donning 'legal observer' hi-vis and taking out notebooks. The crew of the World's End rolled down in matching masks. Someone came dressed as a tiger. We dropped more banners as people arrived.

HOMELESSNESS IS NOT A CRIME.

We put a little sound system up to the window of the second floor and Spike started deejaying old school hip-hop to the people below. We organised a rope-ladder so people could climb up and join us inside. We threw money down and sent someone to the shop to buy beers.

EVERY TIME YOU EVICT A SQUAT, A KITTEN DIES.

Peals of laughter from below. I was manic. I kept changing

clothes, going from anarcho-black-bloc to a wedding dress and Lucha Libre mask, unsure of whether I should be making a joke of this or not.

A passerby paused to take a photo. It must have looked like the opening credits of the *Muppets Show* done by the Zapatistas. Osmond dropped his banner with perfect timing.

MOVE ALONG. NOTHING TO SEE HERE.

The bailiffs arrived, maybe three or four of them, and a police car too. They got out and spoke to someone downstairs. We hung out the windows with our hearts in our throats. Just the other week bailiffs had made a dash for the door despite the masses of people there to protect the space. You never knew.

We dropped the last banner — a simple, gigantic black 'A' within a circle.

I watched from the second floor, ready to rush downstairs to brace the barricade on the front. The bailiffs were looking at the mass of black masks with some amusement.

After a few moments, the bailiffs got back in the car and left. The police went off to a barrage of cat-calls and oinking noises.

We had won.

World's End

The first step in the evolution of ethics is a sense of solidarity with other human beings.

— Albert Schweitzer

'Don't evict Christmas!'

Two days before the world's most famous squat-baby celebrated his 2013th birthday, the squat in Camden opposite the World's End was scheduled for a visit from the High Court enforcers. By some trick of wrangling, the occupants had received notice of the date pinned to their metal door, and the call-out for support had been made.

It is highly unusual to get prior notice of the visit of High

Court enforcers. County Court bailiffs post notice, usually allowing up to six weeks before they come, and after that it is handed over to the High Court, should the CC fail to evict. High Court enforcers then arrive without notice, once endorsed by the Court.

Everyone turned up, 8am, ready for action. The SQUATTERS RIGHT OR SQUATTERS RIOT banner hung from the top floor of the three storey, manned by black masks. Atop the next door bank building, someone had climbed up to a dizzying precipice and hung the black flag and squat logo. It fluttered threateningly over oblivious commuters hustling to the underground. Anarcho punk of scratchy guitars and screeching angry voices blasted from an open window upstairs, spiced with flashes of jungle.

We collected a mattress down the road and dragged it half a mile to flop it down onto the pavement. Grimy masked punks immediately dropped on to it, leaning against the wheelie bin that had been positioned in front of the door. More of them plonked on top, relaxed and ready, looking out over the assembling mob.

A man in an embroidered Japanese robe and topknot was dipping a length of rope slung between two canes into a bucket of foam. As he removed it, he held it up to the wind and a bubble four metres long blossomed from between the ropes. Swollen and glistening it rose upwards and above Camden, floating past the flickering squat-flag atop the bank. A woman dressed all in red, with skulls blazoned on her stockings and an elf-hat on her head, fluttered around the crowd, popping bubbles and comically leaping into the air to catch them. She was chatting with the smiling faces and glowering masks, offering tea and croissants to whoever wanted.

A guy in full orange hi-vis, the jacket encrusted with oily black filth, staggered about between the bikes and smiles, his face hidden by a peacock coloured Lucha Libre mask. He smoothly collected the beer can from a dapper-dressed elderly gentlemen who could no longer contain his excitement, and pissed at length in the doorway of the World's End. I knew the gent from Hackney and before, an old boy on the scene who'd tell tales of the Squatter's Union of the 70s, and how he spent most of his time in the RAF frequenting brothels and drinking Mai Tais. We would be there only one hour, and he would go three times, flooding the doorway and the pavement with piss.

A squat-priest in dog collar and executioner's mask was conducting a sermon on a step in a doorway, offering benedictions and blessings to the crowd, calling on the God of Squatting to grant strength to those inside, and to shrink the testicles of the bailiffs.

Floating serenely around with a Staffy terrier on a leash, a woman in a black mask daintily picked up the billowing skirts of her wedding dress to avoid the stream pouring into the road, revealing battered Converse sneakers underneath. There were several dogs running around, and the Bride was careful to control and monitor her own dog's interactions with them.

The tension was palpable. Already people were drinking and the raucous laughter and hooting beginning in certain sections. People made solidarity fists up at the windows where masked eyes peeped out curiously. A gang sat on the roof behind the banners, watching and waiting.

The last time we'd been here had been the day after our own resistance at the Place, when the Camden crew had organised a rooftop punk gig for the unappreciative hipsters of North London. We had stood, much like this, waiting at the foot of the building, whilst the crew inside dropped banners in solidarity with the Polycolour squat in Warsaw that had been firebombed by fascists. Several bikers had gone off to hijack the Critical Mass assembly and draw them up en masse to fill the street. Hundreds of people and bikes choked that little side street, though taxis still insisted on trying to plough through as the amps turned on and the punk began to blast down. One Hackney carriage had a skinny mohawked punk run over the top of it even as it was moving, dropping down into the street on the other side without a stumble to the crowd's whooping appreciation.

People grabbed wheelie bins and blockaded the road to prevent further interruptions and potential hit-and-runs.

The bailiffs arrived, bemused. The police approached the

mob, sparking flutters of panic and movement as they saw them coming. Lifting a placating hand, the officer requested a representative to negotiate with them. Someone stepped out of the crowd and wandered over to chat with the owners and bailiffs.

They negotiated for a stay, agreeing to leave voluntarily shortly after New Year. People chatting with the enforcers heard that they had evicted two elderly people the day before, and had bookings right through the Christmas period, even on the day itself.

I couldn't help but wonder what Jesus would have made of it all.

Interlude:
The Red Snapper

It was already after midnight — Sunday morning — before we got the location of the party. Spike and I were lounging around in the cavernous belly of the Kentish Town Place, feeling like Jonah inside the whale. I'd bought a half-gram of coke to keep our energies up, but for a long moment, it looked like our Saturday night adventure was on the brink of dissolution.

Then Spike got the message. His phone was constantly buzzing with calls and updates, but the one we had been waiting for finally bleeped through.

'Dalston. I got the address. My mate is DJing we can get in free. Brooklyn hip-hop. You still up for it?'

I wavered. It was already late. Perhaps this hadn't been the best idea. Spike always came back from his sojourns, days later, wild-eyed and manic, full of stories of dark squat parties and characters from the underbelly of London. The sofas of the Kentish Town Place were grimy yet comfortable. I could just go to bed.

Then we did a bump, and were off.

We strolled through the eerie calm of the backstreets of Kentish Town Road. We took two night buses, buzzing quietly, Spike never off his phone, over to Dalston, where we started walking.

Within minutes, we began meeting clumps of people coming the other way − early bailouts from the party. We used them like a blazed trail, seeking their source. The road lead into a warehouse estate, looming empty monoliths brooding behind wire fencing. Soon, we could feel the thud of bass in the concrete around us. We were close.

We saw a pair of smiling greeters standing in the doorway of a warehouse unit. Pounding music, gaggles of giggling girls wandering in and out. They seemed to beckon. At the door, something went wrong. Spike couldn't get hold of his mate. We had to pay.

Stung by the four quid, we stepped in, relieved that we had at last arrived. Inside, a bar had been built in the corner of one unit, and in the other, three Portacabins were being worshipped by a long line of impatient toilet-goers. Next door, a second unit was full of people dancing a Dalston two-step before a set of massive speakers.

We wandered through, trying to get a feel for the party.

Something didn't sit right. Everyone was very clean, very young, very proper. We looked like a pair of homeless vagabonds. In the smoking area, our attempts to speak to people were met with looks of disgusted mistrust. We were not welcome here. More disconcertingly, the music they were playing sounded terrifyingly like four-on-the-floor house music. Not Brooklyn hip-hop at all.

Whilst Spike went off to find his mate, I approached the bar.

'Three quid fifty.'

'For a can of Grolsch?'

'It's all for a good cause, mate.'

'What cause?'

The guy had to go ask someone what they were raising money for. I carried on smiling and chatting nonsense, boosted by another bump, and in the ensuing confusion, the barman forgot to ask me for any money. After an appropriate amount of chatting, I took the can and sauntered back to find Spike.

He was manic.

'We're at the wrong party man!'

Apparently, there were more than a few warehouse parties in Dalston that night. I laughed it off, cheered by the free beer, and we abandoned the party and set off back into the night. Just outside the door, a woman's voice called.

'Spike! Spike!'

We turned, and a pair of arms wrapped themselves around Spike. A little gnomish woman with brown eyes, brown hair and a brown cap was joyfully greeting and cooing over Spike. He was smiling, happy, amazed, telling her how we were at the wrong party.

'I go to one squat party in Whitechapel. You should come,' she spoke with a lilting Portuguese accent.

Spike looked at me. I shrugged. This seemed fortuitous.

Another two night buses. My Oyster card was taking a pounding, the buses packed with people moving from one party to another, just like us. At least in a squat I might not feel so alienated.

The Whitechapel squat was a huge, cuboid office building of glass and white steel. A bearded man with a bucket stood at the entrance, collecting change for the homeless. I threw in the last of my coppers and hoped he didn't notice. We wound our way up the stairwell to the third floor, hearing furious techno reverberating through the building. Crews of ragged looking people loitered around the stairs. Spike said hello to some of them. I made the conscious decision to follow his every lead here.

Instead of the party, we went into a side room, an old office, where a couple of people Nada (the Portuguese girl) and Spike knew were smoking spliffs.

One ferret-faced occupant was rattling his jaw as we entered.

'It's like chess, man. The hackers make a move, then the government makes a move, and we're waiting to see who wins. But it's getting old man. We had a meeting the other day and there's like one MI5 guy, one from the CIA, and one from Mossad in there. And there's only four people in the meeting.'

People laughed.

Spike was a little shifty in here. He knew the guys, and the talk of surveillance and undercovers never makes people relax in these situations. I wondered what the hell I was getting into.

Then Nada was there, relaxed and smiling, offering a CD cover with four tiny white lines on it. Spike hoovered one up without hesitation. I was a little more cautious.

'What is it?'

'MXE. A ketamine analogue. Think about what you have already taken. It is very powerful. I only sell in half-gram amounts. Point one is the active dose. Point five might kill you. It lasts four hours, then *finito*.'

I loved it when dealers knew their product, and Spike's confidence inspired a devil-may-care attitude. I took the tube, and snorted.

We went through to the party room. Lazers sliced the air and a smoke machine filled the place with psychedelic smog. Techno raged, that furious, alien techno that drives humanity from people. Clusters of people were milling around the empty office space, sitting on carpet, hanging by the DJ booth. The drug began to take to take hold.

I was sweating outrageously, with the urge to remove all my clothes but fearful of being naked and vulnerable in such a strange place. I was struggling with the limits of my perception and sensory overload. My brain felt runny, my body made of dissected pieces of meat that were struggling to work together. I half danced, half staggered around the place, unable to speak, unable to really function, just feeling the raging sonic impact of the music blasting through me as I sweated and babbled and staggered.

On one wall was a huge picture of Harlequin from the Batman series, the sexy masked jester-villain. I stood gob-smacked before her as she writhed and danced sinuously, peeling off her layers of clothing, revealing a taut, muscular body underneath complete with six breasts and a vagina like a steel mantrap.

I was not in that room in Whitechapel. I was in a place of violent colour and infinitesimal fractal detail. For a long while, I battled, reassured by every reappearance of Spike or Nada, who seemed similarly unable to speak, but ultimately happy to be there.

Hours, or maybe seconds, passed, and we were in the corridor, my tongue flapping but only strange, guttural sounds emerging, like I was speaking Elvish. We chopped up the rest of the coke. With numb-faces we decided to brave the outside world.

The Sunday morning sky was a turquoise tarp stretched over the looming spires of the City. We rocked out, suddenly unburdened from the raging techno, still staggering a little from the MXE. Nada set off, leading us up the City Road and onto Brick Lane. The walls there writhed with a mélange of graffiti and mural: a bridge covered with dayglo political slogans, urging us to 'reclaim love'; a giant octopus tangling its tentacles around dozens of wailing people; a tiny scrawl just above the pavement that read, '99% of people will not notice this sign.' The very walls of Shoreditch crawled with shifting waves of paint, each one attacking and overcoming the others, growing and retreating over the buildings like different strains of mould.

I stood on the corner of Sclater Street staring at the giant pink ear that was emerging from one wall, thinking about surveillance, whether *they* could hear us or not. Nada was ringing a door-bell above a minicab firm, telling us that it was where the inventor of Bitcoin lived. I wasn't so sure.

The door remained closed, and we wandered some more. At one point, two guys similarly blitzed on chemical delights rode up on Boris bikes and we swapped madness for a few moments together. I felt creeping paranoia that our obviously enhanced state might attract attention. Again, I followed Spike's lead. He was cool, so I could be too.

We were somewhere on the edge of the City when the drugs

began to lose their hold.

Four hours in, right on schedule, we were coming down from the first hit, the drugs relinquishing their grip. Meandering through the Sunday morning glare of Shoreditch under a blinding azure sky, we made our way through the paint-daubed avenues of Brick Lane to Arnold Circus. Here, a bandstand stood in the centre of a ring of tall trees already flush with the emerald foliage of spring, shielding a whiff-whaff table from the sunshine.

The bandstand was built from the rubble of the Old Nichol slum that used to sprawl across this part of London, forming the centerpiece of the Boundary Estate regeneration project. The Rookery, as it was notoriously known, was one of the many filthy and overcrowded shambles around Whitechapel: roads were unpaved, rambling alleyways, hovels built right on the packed earth. The animal reek of pigs and cows mingled with boiling tripe and melting tallow. Slaughter houses, dustheaps, and lakes of putrefying night soil added to the filth. Now — the scene was serene, green and clean. High up on one of the trees, someone had placed a plaster-cast of the Green Man — his dead eyes watching over us from up in the branches.

Shuffling around in the shade, we waved at the dog-walkers and young mothers wheeling their children around in the fresh air. Spike found a baggie with a crumb of green inside, and we cackled as we wrapped it up in a cigarette, not believing our good fortune. Nada lounged on one of the benches. We quietly gathered ourselves as we processed the monumental confusion and hallucinations of the night-time's revelry. I remembered Arnold Circus from another hedonistic debauch through East London, and the space felt safe and secluded after rambling around Whitechapel. Tall, clean red brick buildings formed comforting cliffs that hugged and held us snug at the convergence of seven roads. A good spot to watch for roving police cars and a powerful centre of confluence.

Nada had to leave, to work as a carer that day. It seemed insane, but she proffered the wrap of white powder with a tired and blissful smile.

'Just take a little bit,' she drawled in the languid long vowels of a Porto native. 'Zero point one is the active dose. Beware the Red Snapper.'

Spike made a tube out of a bus ticket. He sniffed it up, and sat back. Nada and I followed. As it hit my sinus I spluttered, blowing a little powder off into the wind. I glanced over, embarrassed by my poor technique. The others were cuddling on the bench, and didn't notice.

The countdown began, again.

This was a serious drug in a high-visibility scenario. The stakes were as high as we were, and we had to get Nada to the train before it kicked in. The cavalier attitude to such powerful hallucinogens that Nada and Spike sported was inspiring. I was nervous but committed.

We wandered down Chance Street to the Bethnal Green Road, turning off to get to Shoreditch High Street station. Under the railway bridge, overgrown with trees and shrubbery, I paused by the wire fence to examine the padlocks lovers had locked there to symbolise their infatuation. It seemed an unusual symbol. Nada and Spike said a warm, almost intimate ,farewell, and I wondered why he hadn't pressed the matter of her own obvious infatuation with him. Nada then hugged me tightly, and I kissed her cheek, before she disappeared through the barriers back into the sterile underworld.

Spike and I headed back out into the streets, the sunshine blasting, and the querulous tremors of the powder working their way up our spines into our cerebral cortex.

I could feel it coming on strong. I began to feel the bite of the Red Snapper.

Within moments, my legs were distant, spindly objects, and my head felt like a plate balanced on a pair of stilts. The pavement rolled away into infinity, a highway of billowing marshmallow clouds. We tried to shuffle along, but at the precipice of a pavement like a mountaintop our movements stalled, and for a long, long while we were trapped, frozen by the iridescent traffic lights. Sunday morning traffic rolled by lazily like grazing elephants, scooters zipping by like cheetahs. The world began to radically reorganise itself.

Whilst I still had the power of speech, I repeated the two safety rules to Spike, who was wobbling along behind me:

'Don't take your clothes off, and don't start screaming.'

He smiled, a mouth full of jaguar ivory. Somehow we managed to totter to a small paved area, where I gripped a metal handrail, and held on for dear life.

The Snapper boiled up my mind in waves. At times, my body dissipated into atoms and released my mind into the psychogeographical sub-texture of the city. My every thought became manifest, and I worked hard to retain a conscious grip on what I was creating. I saw the construction of buildings, steel girder frames erupting from the road being clad in brick and plaster, roofs blooming like mushrooms, before stripping themselves apart and melting into the road. I understood how I was creating the city, that everything I saw only existed because I looked at it. I saw the walls crawling with lush, green vinery, beans climbing up the drainpipes to sprawl across the windows. Tall fields of barley and corn grew in the roads, city workers in straw hats languidly weeding between the gently ululating waves of yellow stalks.

I tried to verbalise my vision to Spike.

'Pumpkins . . . we should plant lots of pumpkins. This whole area could grow pumpkins.'

Yet even as they clattered out of my mouth the words became alien and weird. I couldn't tell if I had spoken them, or merely thought them, or if there was even a difference. I was aware I was babbling incoherently. Queer looks were being shot my way by shoppers heading off to the markets of Brick Lane. What must they think of me, obviously and publically deranged, fragmented, eyes goggling in my skull, my tongue flapping like a sail in the wind.

I gripped the metal stand tighter, feeling at any moment that I might blast off like a rocket ship into the super-strata of reality. The waves increased in intensity, body turning to mist and mind unleashed. Pumpkins grew to enormous sizes all around us, dense creepers choking off the traffic lights and blocking traffic.

Spike, somehow, was talking to someone on the phone, and in a flash I saw the city organise into violent insurrection – guerilla gardeners storming the banks, casting seed in all directions, gypsy caravans clogging the crossroads and playing vigorous violin jigs whilst the milk maids danced amongst the foraging ducks. We would be on the news already, as arch-villains or folk heroes, our faces blasted a million times across the screens as the instigators of this civil uproar. By the time we were home, teenagers everywhere would be playing a free downloadable game based on our adventures.

I looked at Spike – his chestnut brown eyes went supernova.

'Your eyes are like galaxies.'

He laughed, the waves of joy bursting from him infectious.

Two maniacs laughing deep and hard by the Shoreditch

bridge.

Rallied by the mirth, we set off as determinedly as we could down Great Eastern Street, heading north, beginning our epic journey across London, back to the safety of Kentish Town.

We walked. We marched like psychonauts through London, brazen in our derangement, happy lunatics stomping through the city with our heads wobbling and eyes spinning. Up Great Eastern Street, into Old Street, past the Foundry, still empty after all these years, down to the great circular junction. I laughed, remembering the record store, so long before, and the times at the Foundry where I'd dropped acid and DJed in the street to two hundred rabble rousers who flung chairs at police cars.

On and on, endlessly, we walked. After an age, we found ourselves somewhere in Highbury. It felt like a strand of Middle Earth. Spike was trying to get to another squat, but when we arrived, it was closed to us. All we could do is walk some more. We trekked through Highbury & Islington, laughing at the little hobbits around us, gazing through our own reflections in windows. Our legs wobbled but we rolled on like drunken sailors on the deck of a ship tossed by a raging storm. The sun shone, and we were free.

PART THREE

Well Finished

Someone is chained to this door by the neck. Any attempt to open it is
attempted murder. DO NOT OPEN.

— Sign for defence of Well Furnished

I realised how much I loved Ari when she superglued herself to
the shopfront window.

We reopened Well Furnished after being discovered in the
nearby GP's office on Well Street. It had been a social centre
not two weeks before and illegally evicted by the owner. We
cracked our old furniture shop just in case it happened again —
which it did.

Whilst Duval spent eight hours on a rooftop demanding to
see paperwork from the bailiffs — paperwork which obviously

didn't exist — I engaged in my own one man barricade and sealed myself inside the mouldy old shed which had been Well Furnished three years before. TV celebrity bailiffs from poverty porn show *The Sheriffs are Coming* had a reputation for dodgy paperwork and a slack approach to legality. Legend had it they promised owners they'd evict squatters no matter what and we were determined to not lose out again. I'd screwed the door shut, rammed every stick of furniture I could find up against it and sat out a day waiting for news from the GP as my phone battery slowly died. I was much happier to be inside than on a roof. I slept well behind my solo barricade.

When the others moved over with their stuff from the GP, we set about frenziedly preparing for the sheriffs. Bad timing meant that the builders working over the road had discovered us in the yard within hours of opening. People were going from one resistance to another as if the whole of Well Street was in revolt. Whilst Duval erected a three metre scaffold tower on the crumbling roof of the shed I made warning signs threatening the health and safety of anyone climbing on the roof or opening a door. I was sleeping in the little cupboard room to one side of the building and over the door I secured a d-lock that would fit around my neck when I sat on the floor. They would have to decapitate me to open that door.

I began to wonder if things had gone too far.

The GP's had looked promising. The walls were covered in insurrectionary anarchist propaganda, which for me only added to the charm. It was good that we hadn't relied on the owner not evicting on a Sunday morning. We would all have been out on the street.

But returning to Well Furnished was like falling back through a wormhole in time. The floor that I'd lovingly rebuilt had rotted completely away again and a foot-high mushroom was growing out of it. The place had returned to its previous state of tomblike neglect and there was no trace of the joy and pain and laughter and adventure that had once filled it. Felicity was a boater now. Doc Homerton had moved to sunnier climes. Moleman was having threesomes in Berlin. Tanya having a baby in Australia. The only familiar face was A. and he was struggling.

But Ari was there, hand super-glued to the window, ready to fight for a place just because it was the right thing to do and she could do it. The theory was they couldn't smash the window if people were stuck to it. It took her over an hour to unglue herself with nail polish remover.

The weekend since the eviction had been a catalogue of disasters. We'd screwed up with the Place, gotten too relaxed. Me and Duval went to court on Tuesday but forgot our phones and the claim number. The next day I returned to be informed the high court bailiffs had been booked for the last two weeks. I determined not to panic and rode the bus back thinking furiously. At home there was no one around to inform. Calmly, I gathered my tools and tried to find someone to communicate to. Duval was asleep. A. was at work. Tasha was studying. I couldn't find anyone.

Then Ari came up the winding staircase, her cerulean eyes sparkling with fear.

'There's police inside.'

It wasn't her first eviction — she'd been at the Pigeon Coup — but it was the first time she'd been evicted from anywhere she had stayed in for more than twelve hours. I did my best to reassure her that it was all part of the process, keeping it as cheerful and carefree as possible.

They'd walked up right behind her. Five officers in uniform.

Eyes darting. Postures tense. Waiting for trouble. The yellow-jacketed bailiffs came up after and the owner shuffling behind like a corpse kept moving with a cattle prod.

'OK. We're leaving. Let us take our things and there will be no problem.'

I'd spoken to the owner on the phone before begging him for a deal.

'What you people want is something for nothing. I came to London when I was sixteen and built myself up over the years. You lot should do the same.'

I hadn't the energy or the heart to argue with him, that over half a century ago London had been a very different place.

The boom years had poured money and opportunity over the people of that generation and spoiled them so rotten that in this millennium they had little idea of how different the situation was.

We spent a week barricading the building before Christmas but it was the same story. In the end we just relaxed. The bailiffs came through a Yale lock next to the moveable barricade we had built to keep them out. We weren't soldiers. We were just living our lives. That week we calmed down the drugs and alcohol and started skipping every morning, eating well and being happy. Then the bailiffs came.

We moved — 30 of us — to the nearby squat. I had had a brief but catastrophic affair with one girl staying there. Solidarity means that you help people, even if you don't particularly like them, but begrudging solidarity just feels awkward. I started hunting for houses that night.

At 3am one morning I looked around the table and realised that I was the last one left who knew what the fuck to do. Sick of meetings and arguments I took the boltcroppers I'd bought for eight pounds on the Kentish Town Road — even telling the shop owner exactly what I meant to do with it — and rode off to a pub in Mornington Crescent. My heart in my throat, I snapped the padlocks off the door with an explosion of metal shards and snatched the evidence up guiltily, slinging it into a drain before ringing them to tell them the pub was open.

It meant that we could move out and we spent one last happy Valentine's Day together in the function room, with someone jangling the piano whilst we drank wine and sang songs in the candlelight. We were still cocksure at that point, and even agreed when Duval said we should leave because the owner seemed 'a decent bloke'.

The next day all the bullshit began. Someone overheard someone talking shit about them and I walked into the middle of a raging argument between two crews in the squat. You could drawn a rough line between the Lithuanian crew and the others, but really it was people playing kings and queens. I told them it wasn't personal but pragmatic. Housing ten people was easier than housing thirty. I managed to placate them, but it was not to be the last time personal politics split a crew that should have been pulling together. The twist would be that the Lithuanians would open one place and live there six months unmolested, whereas our route was to be radically less easy.

So the split happened, and we raged on to find another building that Saturday. Ill-advisedly, Osmond and I agreed to do a gig at the local social centre. The speaker didn't work and it was badly organised. Me and Osmond started pounding speed, and I ended my show by screaming, 'GO FUCK YOURSELF' into the microphone.

We opened the GP that night. It took hours and hours and we kept sniffing and climbing and struggling. By the end, I stood holding the crowbar ranting about cracking Well Furnished. To open something. Anything. Just not to be homeless or staying in a squat where people barely spoke to me or each other.

So on the third night we opened Well Furnished. Three nights. Three squats. We weren't going to get thrown out of this one. The tower went up and the glue went on and the associated allies gathered by the big main gate and argued legalities with the bailiffs when they tried to talk us out. Osmond waited out there all day, sleeping on the pavement when he was too tired to stand anymore.

They left us in the mouldy shed, with its rotten floor and black streaked collapsing walls. Within days people were getting sick. Lung infections. Osmond was flagging but still fighting. Still working. Still sniffing.

Ari stayed positive. She was strong and determined and a rock for people to turn to. She helped make the decisions, skipped food and laughed deliriously at the lame jokes we made. We set up a little kitchen table and ate together. We took our happiness when we could, laughing at the effort we had put into defending such an utter derelict shit-hole.

There were ten or more of us and it was all one acoustic unit. We didn't want a social centre anymore. We just wanted somewhere to live. We worked out the logistics of building rooms and making it a shanty town. It wasn't the same. We were stressed, almost broken. The crew had been settled for too long — nine months one building, eight months the next, and then six months in the Place. People had forgotten how stressful opening and barricading can be. People were starting to come apart. They wanted their lives back, not to be constantly at war with owners and bailiffs and police.

Then we got a call from another crew down in Shoreditch. We had helped one of them out before and he had never forgotten us. They had a huge old warehouse building with enough room for everyone, a whole factory unit each. Me and Osmond visited and returned so excited that we were possibly overwhelming in our enthusiasm. A window of opportunity had opened for us and we were keen to go through it.

We found some others who'd been evicted recently and gave them Well Furnished. They were former members of the GP social centre collective. The eviction had shattered their crew as well and there were only three of them left. Well Furnished was perfect for them. It would last another six weeks quite peaceably.

We collected our things and moved en masse to Preacher Street in the heart of E1, into the building we would come to call Squatopolis. It would be there that all that love for Ari would become like ash at the end of a crack pipe.

Amphetanarchy

Amphetamines are the most American drug. You get so much done.
You look terrific, and your middle name is Accomplishment.

— Chuck Palahniuk

The papers arrive at Squatopolis within days of us moving there.
The countdown to eviction starts all over again.

A seven night storm over the barrios of East London. Scramble
over walls, dodge irate neighbours and police cars. Gunter —
fresh-faced ginger Berlin dreadhead — and I look at a Sitexed
pub, the Nadir, across the canal. Park the bikes and jump a
rickety fence, poke around the back ledge, test the Sitex key
against the bolts. Make sure we have the right one.

I hear someone on the phone down below me.

' . . . seems to be someone on the roof of a building, don't know what he's doing up there . . . '

Freeze. Seconds to decide, or be trapped up here. A glance of a civilian male, talking earnestly into his phone and looking straight at me. Drop out of sight, down on my knees. Review. The garden fence. The other side. Hide down the back alley. Trap myself in a dead-end, or freeze here and hope no-one comes.

Not options. Sitex key. Roof. Witness. That is 'going equipped'. The jovial parlance of legality. A night in the cells. Hard questions with no comment or answer.

Adrenaline and the survival instinct take over. Stand. Scramble down the stairs and jump the fence like a springbok. Land less than a metre away from the man on the phone. Glance away.

'No worries mate, just looking for a place to take a shit.'

Not even a smile. I start back to where the bikes are parked with Gunter. He stares blankly, awaiting information.

'Unlock the bikes and let's bust. That fucker is snitching.'

We fuddle with the locks, suddenly all thumbs, such cheap crap. Why did I never oil the lock? Why did I always struggle each time, cursing it, and now it was going to get me arrested and — ah, there it went. The snitch looms across the street, staring at us with accusing eyes. Barely minutes. The locks come away. We shove them into the baskets, saddle up and set off.

At the first junction, I look back. Gunter is gone.

'Fuck.'

His first week in London. His first time squatting. Just abandon him? No. Solidarity and that. At least I knew I'd taken the time to explain 'no comment' interviews to him. But he is so sweet. Could he hold up to ten hours in a cell? Did he know how to demand water until the guards turned off the buzzer? There was so much to learn.

The snitch continues talking. I look desperately up and down for Gunter's little pixie face.

The police car pulls up. Hit the pedals and roll down into the shadows of the canal network, out of there as fast as the wheels can spin me.

'Snitches get stitches, fucker!'

The sound echoes hollow under the canal bridge as I flee.

Gunter turns up at the next junction. Relief. Sitex tool burns a hole in my pocket. We burn rubber back to Preacher Street. The relative safety of Squatopolis.

*

Second night. Dalston. Old building. Seriously derelict. Pigeon shit streaking the walls. Duval wants to try and get in around the back for a closer look. We retire to the opposite side of the canal to watch his progress. Duval maybe not competent, but he certainly is enthusiastic.

'Here — hold my phone. I don't want to lose it if I fall in the canal.'

Like watching a live version of some 1980s 8-bit platform game. Tinny midi-music blasting in my ears. The pixel moon shines on the black waters of the canal. Cans of Polish lager in hand. Duval begins level one.

First, he vaults over the iron railings on the bridge, drops himself down into the narrow gardens behind offices backing on to the canal. Springs over one fence, two fences, comes to a well lit yard, with an office full of people inside. Hesitates. Picks his moment. I can almost hear him say, 'fuck it'. Jumps another fence, bold as brass, strolls over to jump another, and another. He is on a roll, ducking under some wiring and finding himself at the neighbouring building. Hanging on to the fencing, he begins to scale his way along a narrow ledge towards the castle.

He reaches a ledge of moss covered crumbling rock. He hesitates.

People begin to emerge from the illuminated office he's rambled past, looking earnestly in both directions, trying to spot who or what has breezed by, moments before. They hold wine glasses and laugh in a casual bray, the murmur of disturbed cattle. They keep coming in and out, looking, looking, looking.

Duval is frozen. He can't make it the final ten metres without risking falling in. He is faltering.

There is a long moment where we see him trapped, waiting, stuck, like watching Spiderman shit himself on the side of a building.

Then, in the car park beyond. Someone emerges from an office, and the huge iron gates beyond begin to pull open.

Duval never misses a beat. He pulls himself over the wire-mesh fence. Drops into the car park. A leisurely stroll, makes his way through the carpark, out on to the other side. Completely hidden from the scouting office workers he spooked earlier.

Game over.

*

Night number three, we try south of the river. University House. Right on Borough High Street. Rolling over to examine it feels like crossing into a foreign country. South has its own flavour, even in Borough. We cruise over Tower Bridge. I look out towards Westminster — the looming single-eye of the Millennium Wheel gleaming on the waters. Think about all the wealth and power concentrated around this body of water: the silver peaks and pinnacles of the City behind us, ringed by its guardian dragon statues, patrolled by its autonomous police force. Us — little rats scurrying through looking for holes to nest in.

Perro, the punk with the two-foot orange mohawk who'd run over a car at the World's End, had been talking about this place since the Battle of Well Street. It sounded too good to be true.

'We used to e-squat one place e-south of the river. In Boorow. A e-school. We stay there three month. They give deal. Is nice place. E-showers. Many room. We can open it for you. It is easy.'

Perro and the Galician punks stand on the street right outside the front door, flamboyant mohawks hidden under black hoods, pierced lips smuggled into ratty scarves. Backpacks and facemasks. Me, Duval, Gunter, Ari and A., all too aware that we are begging a favour off of them, but they are happy to help. They see what we are going through. We wait by the door, pretend to wait for a bus. The punks disappear.

'How long do you think this is going to — '

The heavy wooden doors swing open. A punk grins at us from inside.

We scramble through the door, hear Perro say to bewildered passerbys as we enter, 'No worry, we have e-squat the place. Is all legal. If police come, you esplain dat. OK?'

The door slams. Duval immediately sets about screwing the locks, finding pieces of wood and metal to barricade it shut.

Others begin to move through the gutted building. Motes of dust choke the air and vast sections of the flooring are missing.

Four storeys, obviously in the midst of refurbishment, and at every corner, there is a suspicious, alien sphere, suspended on a pole. On each floor, large, android-looking devices like crude dildos for gigantic aliens have been bolted to metal plates.

The devices begin to talk:

'You have illegally entered this building. The police are on their way. You will be prosecuted for breaking and entering . . . '

We've dealt with alarms before. That was nothing to worry about. Then A. points out.

'These things are cameras.'

The spheres on every corner are little security cameras, recording our every antic. Rather than panicking, we keep to the plan. Unscrew each one and collect them in a metal box. All the time, as I wander around, more and more doubts about this place.

'Didn't you say this place was full of asbestos?' asks Duval.

'No, just one or two rooms,' answers Perro. 'But they have completely destroyed the place. There was floor. There was door. There was light and shower . . . and now . . . '

'You have illegally entered this building. The police are on their way . . . '

A. is not impressed. 'We can't stay in a place with asbestos, man. That shit is toxic.'

People start donning the dust masks scattered around. As we look through the signs and paperwork, we can't find any evidence of asbestos being mentioned but then, BANG! BANG!

BANG!

'Open up in there! Who are you? What are you doing?'

Duval is first to the barricades, sitting on a length of wood to further jam it behind the door.

'We have legally occupied this building! We did not damage anything coming in. This is a civil matter between us and the owner of the building.'

'We have witnesses saying you broke in. Come out now.'

Duval motions to the cameras. 'Witnesses,' he mutters. 'They've been watching us on these things. They haven't got shit.'

'That place is dangerous it's full of asbestos,' opines another voice from outside.

Duval whispers to us, 'Go around and make sure they aren't trying to get in from any other window.'

We begin scurrying around checking doors and windows — all bolted and barred. Find the rooftop window Perro has entered through — undamaged and unbroken — simply left open for when he needs it.

Get back down. Duval is leaning out a second floor window chatting amicably through his mask with the police and security guards.

'Yeah we arrested someone for breaking in here just last week,' a policeman is saying.

'Well we didn't break in. The window was open,' responds

Duval, like a neighbour chatting over the garden fence.

'Well, it's their death if they want to stay.'

Crude psychology, or genuine fact, it's impossible to know. We keep scrambling around looking for information, but nothing reads asbestos. In the basement we find several thousand pounds worth of tools: angle grinders, a generator, top class hammers and circlesaws, a prybar, a veritable treasure trove of equipment. I stand over it, the possibilities whirring in my head. I make a mental inventory. Run back up to check on Duval and the others.

'Can we have our alarms back?' asks the security guard.

Dutifully, we go around, lifting the weird android blocks into a bucket we found. Gunter makes some elaborate rope system of knots, ties off the basket. Duval and A. lower it down out the window. The sound of its alarm diminishes plaintively.

'You have illegally entered this building, the police . . .'

The tension begins to disperse. If they are taking the alarms, it means they had surrendered for this part. The building is ours.

We smoke and wave goodbye to the authorities, turning around to survey our prize.

'Guys, I don't think we can stay here. There's no water, electrics or floors. How desperate are we?' asks A. It's a great question.

'It's the asbestos that bothers me.'

'There's no asbestos, they're just trying to fuck with us and make us leave . . . '

'We could get a deal here.'

'A deal? It's in worse condition than the mouldy shed we lived in . . . '

The bickering begins. The speed begins to flag. The adrenaline draining out. Me and Ari go upstairs, climb out the window on to the rooftop. The night air is cool, clear and balmy. All around us Borough sings with the clamour of revellers. Sirens wail, reassuringly distant and diminished. The City gleams across the water. We look back to where Squatopolis waits, nestled alongside Brick Lane. Less than half a mile from the Shard, which looms apocalyptically above us, an ivory tower of illusory wealth and real disparity. I'd read recently that most of it was empty, unsold, and awaiting speculators to move in and fill it.

Me and Ari laugh about squatting a floor in there, opening it up in suits and high heels, setting up a squatter's estate agents, with pictures of all the empties and the land registry details on hand for prospective occupants.

A. and Duval come up. A long moment of calm.

'So, we are leaving?' asks Gunter.

'We can't stay here. It's worse than a fucking shanty town,' says A.

'It's a lot of work. But we could get a deal,' I say.

'Or we could get an IPO tomorrow,' says Duval, ever the optimist.

We look around. We learn some buildings just aren't worth fighting for. Despite the time limit on Squatopolis, it is still more comfortable than this.

Before we leave, I take Duval and A. back down to the basement to look over the haul of tools.

'Imagine what we could do with these. There must be a thousand pounds worth of kit here. We haven't got anything.'

'All our tools have been tatted. Between the Place, Well Street and here, we've lost nearly everything,' says A. I love the way he purrs the r's on his words, like a jungle cat.

'You can't take these,' says Duval. 'These belong to the workmen. They obviously finished work today or yesterday. These belong to them. You can't rip off the workers. They normally aren't even insured.'

It is hard, looking over all that kit. The others go back upstairs, prepare to bail. I decide that if they can afford to leave them here, they can afford a few losses. A roll of gaffer tape. A heavy iron prybar with a beautiful curved end. Shove it down my trousers, join the others by the door.

'Someone wake up the dog.'

Perro is asleep in a chair, his boots stacked on top of each other, face buried in his scarf. Someone claps in his face. He wakes up, rubbing his eyes with knuckles tattooed with ACAB.

'Vamonos?'

'Si, si, let's go.'

Assemble by the door, a headcount, crack off the barricades and unlock the Yale. Step quickly out into the night. On the street, pass the prybar in a scarf to Ari to take back to Shoreditch on the bus. Jump the bike and ride home empty handed.

*

The fourth night. Try closer to home. Every attempt precursored by shambolic meetings attended by drunken, exhausted caricatures of people I used to know. We keep collecting more miscreants who sneak their way in and set up shop at our kitchen table. A. tells them to fuck off so we can talk business. I wake around 6pm. Out into the kitchen to scavenge from the skipped food. Gunter and Ari were Germanically fastidious in collecting sushi from the local Wasabis, checking the Tesco bin hourly for drop-offs of black bananas and stale bread. A. keeps riding up bags of day-old sandwiches from Eat.

Even Osmond, collapsing under the stress of his amphetamine addiction still manages a bag of super-sweet cupcakes from the bakery every now and then. People keep disappearing, coming back sniffing and wide eyed as the cheap speed hits their bloodstream. Those who aren't into powder cane sugar in massive doses. Everyone drinks pints of tea, keeps cracking cans of Okocim or Tyskie. My nose is constantly running. My heart pounds. I don't know how we keep coming to decisions. I

I am committed to action, not theory.

The Colony — a huge, grade-II listed building visible from the doorway of Squatopolis. Squatted a couple of times before. Can easily house dozens of people, if in relative squalor. The mysterious processes of group-decision making. We decide.

Me and A. out at dusk, look and stare and wonder at how to get in. The building is huge — a towering monument to waste and emptiness, four storeys peaking in beautiful sloping gables of some design of architecture I wished I knew the name of.

Walking around and around, we debate putting a ladder up to the second floor window. We take the boltcroppers, walk down to the padlocked door. People stream past between Aldgate East and Shoreditch. A. attempts to fit the croppers around the locks. The angle is too tight. I shield him with my scrawny body. Eyeball the burger shack opposite, the car wash beside it. He trys to cut. It isn't happening.

We walk back. A Jaguar pulls up. Two geezers peer out at us.

'Are you all right mate?'

I am shocked. I sniff a block of speed out of one nostril and spit. 'Yeah. Why wouldn't I be?'

'What's that in your hand?'

All alarms ringing. Who the hell are these guys? They look coked up.

'It's my phone. What do you want?'

'Is he with you?' the guy in the passenger seat points at A.

'Yeah, he's my mate.'

'What are you doing here?' he spits at A., the boltcroppers hidden under his army jacket.

'Nothing, just walking home. What do you want?'

A tense moment. The Jaguar geezer breaks it.

'Fucking Somali cunt, why don't you fuck off back to your own country?'

'Ah just fuck off man — '

An image of A. jumping up on the hood of the car and driving the boltcroppers through the windshield into the guy's throat, cleanly snipping his spinal cord with the satisfaction of a padlock shattering. A. doesn't drink because it sets off his temper. I hope he's sober.

'Ah, fuck you guys!'

Start moving away, hope he will follow. The Jaguar burns rubber and rolls off towards the Commercial Road, abuse pouring from the window.

Keep walking, mind spinning, wondering if they are going to come back for us. A streetfight would certainly alleviate some tension, but how to explain the boltcroppers? We go back to Squatopolis. Reconsider.

*

Next night, routine set. Wake up late afternoon, force tea and sugar and sushi into my body, a couple of bumps, go out to find who's around to try again.

A plan. The Colony backs on to a pub with a terrace on top of a high walled roof. Boost up on to that, pull the others up, use the ladder they conveniently store there to climb up the further twenty-five metres on to the roof.

Absolutely ludicrous to me, but, hell, I'm just happy to not to be in charge of this shambles of crooked clowns.

So off we go. Casual stroll down the thirty metres to where the Colony looms. Boost Duval up. He pulls himself up a drainpipe and on to the roof. A. goes next, struggling with his heavy frame. Finally, I climb up. I am drunk. More Polish lager than Japanese food. The mixture has made me heady.

Up on the roof, a little plateau surrounded on three sides by the soaring walls of the pub and the Colony. There is the ladder. I look at the distance Duval intends to climb. Now is not the moment to be overthinking these things.

Dutifully, we begin to unfold the ladder, extending it and moving it into position.

A door on the roof terrace I failed to notice suddenly bursts open. A drunken old woman stands staring at us. Her eyes are rolling, her hands defiantly propped on her withered hips.

'What are you doing?'

Already moving. Put the ladder back down and jump off the edge. Old ladies are much more intimidating than security.

Security tend to be sober.

'Oh, nothing love, we just locked ourselves out of the flat over the road.' Duval's snappy response.

She is confused, bewildered as to why two skinny white punks and a large black man are manhandling her ladder on her rooftop. I see her defences kick in as she rallies her gin-addled senses. By that point I'm already heading down the stairs to the Yale door back on to the street. I hear her haranguing Duval and A. as I leave.

'Get out of here! Get out! I'm calling the police!'

The ladder clatters back down, Duval makes soothing noises. A. stalks down the stairs behind me. Bizarre, Duval doesn't use the stairs and jumps off the terrace edge, swinging off the drainpipe to land remarkably gracefully on the pavement, smooths out his suit jacket, and join us for the short walk of shame back. We can't have been out more than twenty minutes.

'Nice plan, Duval.'

'I'm just trying mate, I'm just trying.'

*

Night number six. Eviction day is looming. In the frenzy I acquire a gram of cocaine, wrapped in a twenty quid note. Spontaneously decide it is the appropriate tool to fuel tonight's action. My face numb and my senses buzzing, I meet the others in the kitchen. Discuss how to crack the Colony.

Squatopolis houses the crew that used to squat the Colony. We have a chat, they inform us that around the back, just beyond where we were the night before, is a large metal grid that covers a hole down into the basement. We assemble our tools, do a head count, and set off.

Ari, A., Gunter, Perro and a Hungarian stoner called Ciba want to join in. We make our way back to the wall of the terrace. The others loiter nearby. A. boosts me up the wall to where we were busted by the drunken landlady the night before. The ladder is still there. Quickly, I follow the wall around the corner, and there is the pit — a five metre drop down onto a steel mesh ceiling covering a gloomy dungeon below. Go back, down the stairs, unlock the Yale door.

Others pile in. As silently as possible, we march up the stairs, eyeing the door where the lady-dragon had burst from the night before, head to the pit.

The pit has the walls of the Colony on two sides, fence next to it leading to other rooftops of the houses and flats on that block. Lower the ladder with abrupt clanking down on to the metal grid, begin poking around, looking for how to open it.

Ari, Perro and me wait at the top. Ciba looks as wild and feral as I feel, eyes constantly searching. Coke rages in me. Sniff constantly, heart pounding. Begin to doubt.

Suddenly inspired. Edge along the top of the pit. Pull myself over the fence to the otherside. Other roof has a huge overgrown bush covering one side. Push myself through to another roof. Use the drainpipe, lever up another level. Feel like Super Mario after eating the star with the smiley face: fucking invincible. At the top of the next platform is a coil of razorwire. With the utmost care, push sleeves down gently on it, lift my booted feet up to the drainpipe to climb higher. To the left — the back windows of various flats and apartments, some lit up by kitchen lights, others reassuringly dark.

One more level, on the sloped, tiled roof of the Colony. This bit is trickier. Slope is steep, tiles loose. Pause a moment, considering. Along one side of the roof is a raised edge, about two foot. If I hang on to the ledge and place my feet flat against it, I can sidestep shuffle up the slope to the apex of the roof.

The trick is total, meditative focus. Forget about falling, maybe you can fly. Don't even count time, muscles strain but feel strong, powered by Peruvian powder, like the ropes of a suspension bridge. Feel like a Hopi native infiltrating the fortresses of the conquistadors.

At the apex, sit, catch my breath, legs straddling the roof.

The view is spectacular — never been higher — the vast stretch of warehouses that houses Squatopolis further down Preacher Street, hear the faint roll of bass from Brick Lane. In the distance, the Royal Hospital gleams where still in use, middle section dark and abandoned. Signs of austerity. The East

London Mosque shoots minarets into the black sky. The other way is the City, sparkling like Oz, and to the north, the rambling lanes and streets of Hackney and beyond.

Now, the descent. Not to fuck up, not to slip and plummet to my death on the pavement four storeys below. I am a fuck-up but this is not my night to die. Boots to the wall, finger tips clinging to the concrete, shuffle inexorably, slowly, down the slope, step by agonising step, to the level where the highest windows of the Colony are.

Investigate. None of them are open. One of them has a wooden board nailed over it. Rattle it. Possible.

Take a deep breath. Shuffle back up the roof, to the top, down the other side.

By the time I arrive I'm breathing hard, sweating. Like a ninja, I clamber back down towards the razor wire. Hear a voice.

'Jorge?'

Freeze. Perro, peers up at me from the lower level, scarf hiding everything but his chestnut eyes, now black in the darkness, like two pools of oil.

Hiss at him.

'I've found the access. I need the crowbar.'

He nods. Disappears. Bushes rustle. Happens twice, Perro returns, holding the iron bar. Passes it up to me.

Beckon for him to follow.

'The wire. I can't climb over the wire.'

Smile. In my pocket is the only tool I thought to bring: a brand new pair of wirecutters. With the skill and satisfaction of an accomplished surgeon, clip the razor wire loops and gently separate them, opening a gap for him to climb up through. Grab his wrist, pull him up.

Now, to climb back over the roof with a crowbar in one hand. give a silent prayer to Quetzalcoatl and thank him for the strength of the Andes.

Crowbar clenched in one fist, one hand only hanging on to the ledge, walk myself up to the top of the roof and look down. A. is down there, a tiny black ant in army camouflage, back on the street heading to Squatopolis. He is alone. He looks up and seems for a moment to see me.

He walks away. A police car. Two police cars. An unmarked undercover vehicle pull up, lights flashing. Can't see the others.

Calmly as I can, signal to Perro to wait. Climb down the roof to sit next to the boarded up window.

Sit and wait. Feel very safe, in control. No way the police are going to climb all this way up, no chance they will even spot me. Just sit tight. Occasionally peep over the edge, watch uniformed officers and a couple of undercovers moving to and fro. The door to the back terrace is open. Hope they will be OK. Control my breathing, count exhalations, half expect to see Gunter and Ciba and Ari get lead out in cuffs at any moment. At least A. is out and clear.

Look up at the moon, bright and full and smiling amongst stars battered into retreat by the blaze of London's light. Look out over the streets and reminisce of other rooftops, other times.

It all seems rather fun, like urban rambling. At least we're getting somewhere. This is good training for all would-be urban guerillas.

After ten minutes, the unmarked car rolls off. I try to remember its design and colour for future protection. Then one more squad car leaves, sirens blaring, then another. We are alone.

Whisper for Perro. He scrambles over, mimicking my style. It takes long minutes. Watch calmly trying not to picture him slipping and tumbling down over the edge. Knocks a couple of slates and they clatter down the rooftop to smack crisply against the brickwork.

Once he is here, I point to the board. He nods.

Try one end, then the other, then the first again. Turn the crowbar one way, then another. There is no purchase. Try to work out the physics of pressure and force, as I've seen others do.

'If I insert here, and lever like this, the pressure goes this way . . .'

'Maybe just e-smash the window,' says Perro.

'But the noise . . . '

Hesitate. Swing the crowbar at the window in a gentle practice, working out the angles like a fisherman casting into the river. Remember Vassily, and another window, so many houses before. Briefly wonder where he is now.

Down on the street, hear the murmur of a giant garbage truck as it grazes its way down Preacher Street like some mechanical megafauna. Perro's black eyes light up. Points at the glass window next to the board.

'Do it! Fucking do it now!'

Adrenaline surging, swing, just as the garbage truck is closest, loudest. Window explodes in a tinkling shower of shards, glass falls down the roof and drops twenty metres to land on the back of the garbage truck. Evidence disappears slowly down the road. Perro and I bundle into the Colony.

Been here before, years ago, just after Well Street had been evicted. Me and A. had gone riding around East London trying to find people and places. Visited here, at that time, they had had a few lightbulbs on, gave it the feel of some vast mine carved into a mountain. Cavernous didn't do it justice. Each floor rambled on and on in every direction, corridors looping and twining around themselves, stairways disappearing up and down into oblivion.

Me and Perro scout the place, assessing the possibilities. Very quickly it begins to remind me of the University School. Yes, it is huge, but it is totally fucked up. Or maybe I am.

Make our way down to the basement, get lost several times and missing the various turns. We get there, the smell of shit and sewage hits us, and along one side of the vast dungeon we see a muffin top of effluent crudely barricaded to prevent it flooding the whole place.

Find the wire net, look up, see Ciba, Gunter and Ari hiding against one wall. Can hear the drunken landlady, somewhere up above them, squarking indignantly to some neighbour.

'They were here last night! I don't know what they want! The police came again but they can't do anything! Why do they keep coming back! ONE OF THEM WAS BLACK!'

Takes a moment for me to realise that the three of them are hiding, have been hiding even before the police arrived. Me and Perro have dodged being trapped up there by minutes. Chuckle to myself. It's good to have these experiences. Makes it more real.

Look at the inside of the door me and A. had tried to boltcrop from the outside the other night. After all the excitement, feel genuine relief and comfort to be inside somewhere. Our little fortress. Door is a huge, a ten-foot wooden monster. Lock just a Yale, takes only minutes to dissemble. Swing it open, see the metal monster installed outside with the padlocks. No way to undo it without the entire metal frame coming crashing down into the street, leaving us defenceless. Bolt the wooden door from inside, look for other options.

Another door, below street level. Begin laboriously unscrewing bolts so we can open it. On the other side is yet another metal frame, but above, we can see a gap where you can get out on to the street. At least, if you're super skinny.

Getting late. Regret not saving some of the cocaine. Body is beginning to shut down. Dust and stench of the building clogging my lungs. Mind befuddled, confused by exhaustion and the diminishing returns of the stimulants packed into it.

'Shit man, do we even want to live here? The basement is full of shit.'

'Yes, but would take a long time to fill up.'

'I think they stripped this place after the last eviction. It's pretty fucked.'

Perro shrugs.

Go back to the dungeon and whisper up to the three people trapped there. Listen for the neighbour. All quiet. They smile at us, thumbs up.

'The police have gone. Go back to Preacher Street and get some tools.'

'They were looking for us with flashlights,' whispers Ari, exhausted but excited still. 'How could they miss us?'

Smile, too tired to respond. Watch them climb up.

From then energy flags, grow more tired, begin discussing and arguing about what to do. Do we get an angle grinder and cut the locks? Do we unbolt the side door? Do we need more people?

Begins to get light outside. In the end, we just run out of

energy.

Perro is slim enough to climb out the side gap. I try, but to no avail. My chest is too thick. He tries to encourage me, but I have nothing left.

He goes back, to get food, water, help, fuck knows. I run around in the Colony, banging my feet and gibbering incoherently to myself. Emtombed in my own squat. I could live like a hermit here. Fuck all these other people. I could be the Ghost of Preacher Street.

Running out of time. If I stay here much longer on my own I could be dealing with security coming to check in the morning. Window might be obvious from the street, even though we'd covered it with a board.

Find a little room with a square hole in one end, through which sunlight is now streaming. I stick my head out. It's raining.

It's an open hole, right above the main gate, maybe fifteen metres up the building. Looking down, there is Ari and Perro with a long length of blue rope.

'I'm fucking trapped.'

They throw the rope up. Already too late for me. All I can see is my doomed attempt to rope myself down on to the gate, clambering over the masonry, slipping and dropping to the pavement, maybe a shattered ankle, maybe a shattered skull. They made it sound so simple, but rope climbing was never my thing.

'Fuck it.'

Bundle the rope, chuck it back out the hole. Raging with the last focus of energy, go back upstairs, the boarded window. Still conscious enough to fit it back behind me, back out on the roof, now in full daylight of the morning, shuffle sidestepping back up to the apex. Slide down the other side, barely catch myself at the first ledge, then back through the cut razor wire, through the bush, on to the terrace on the back of the pub. Storm down the stairwell, unlock the Yale, and back out into the street — just another civilian.

Ari and Perro collect me at the corner of Preacher Street and we stroll back to Squatopolis.

'We were hiding for nearly an hour. How could they not see us? They shone a light right at us.'

A. opens the big metal door for us.

'Man, there was beautiful moment when you were up on the roof, the crowbar raised, just your shadow against the full moon. Awesome work man.'

'Still no place to live though.'

High five. As our hands come away, see A.'s fingers covered with fresh blood.

'Shit man, your hand.'

Only then notice I have a big cut across my fingers, blood all over myself. Wound is covered with dust and grime. Hadn't even felt it.

*

Seventh night. Sit around the Squatopolis kitchen table having breakfast beers and sushi. Someone has made soup, which I manage to squeeze into my stomach. Looking around for who has the speed.

Duval says, 'I think we should go back to the Nadir. I checked it last night. I got most of the screws off the backdoor Sitex.'

I had wondered where he had gone. Too exhausted to care. My hand throbbing. Drink more to get through the pain.

'I was there last night. You can hear the hydroponics flushing in and out in a cycle. Like a washing machine. I bet it's a fucking grow room.' Duval has a great imagination, and he speaks of everything with such conviction.

'It's not a grow room,' I say.

'No listen, right. We checked this place out. It was closed two months ago because the owner was running an illegal hostel there. The place has a reputation for dealing drugs over the bar. The guy who owns it is some Nigerian businessman. I bet you it's a grow room.'

There is so much wrong with that scenario don't know where to begin. Duval is a master arguer, a born debater. In no shape to take him on.

'Fine. Whatever. You guys go do it. I'm knackered. I've been out every night for a week doing this shit. I'm done.' Am on a comedown, feel bleak.

'But I can't find my way there. I'm crap with directions.'

Sometimes can't believe the people I live with. Sigh, rubbing the bandage Nurse Dre had wrapped around it that morning after her night shift.

'For fuck's sake. OK.'

An agonising delay whilst Duval unties the rachet strap. I wait as patiently as I can.

'Is that really necessary? Can we fucking go already?'

'We might need it.'

I scoff. It seems ludicrous, but I wait anyway until he collects it.

A. is also in, bless him. He's been working everyday, and still is committed. The guy is solid.

So we saddle up, Duval, A. and me, and tell the others to be ready to come take over in the morning. Ride off through the night time streets, scuttle past the hordes of people heading out for a night around Shoreditch, up Great Eastern Street, over the canal, and back to the Nadir.

It sits on the corner, just over the bridge, opposite the school.

Seems like a year since I'd been up on that roof. Only five nights. Or seven. Who fucking knew anymore. What a week.

The three of us make our plan.

Duval first, slips over the fence with the Sitex key. Me and A.

sit kicking our heels next to the school. In a minute, the missed call comes through on the phone. Over we go.

Behind the fence is a convenient bin positioned as a barricade for us to drop on to. Slip through the cluttered yard and find him down a flight of stairs, next to a sheet of Sitex. Pull together, cramped awkwardly, we pull back the Sitex. As we pull, hear the repeated whirring and flushing of water coming from inside. For a moment wonder if Duval was right. Perhaps we are about to break into someone's grow. But you need access to that kind of set up regularly, to monitor mould and growth. Not everything can be done on a timer.

The Sitex peels back like a silver skin. Behind it, a door with a Yale. Get the crowbar, work out the pressure points and the angles of force. Slot the bar into the frame, lever together, get access, slide it down closer to the lock.

Check our scenario: we're totally sheltered here, not even neighbours can see down to where we are. Put the drill in position, ready for the lever to seal us in.

Work at the lock, lean into the door. Squeeze in with them, the heady musk of squatter men filling that little alley as we lean, and lean, and lean.

The doorlock pops satisfyingly. We are in.

Me and Duval storm in, A. waits outside ready to lock us in.

In the basement. All the lights are on. A hostel reception area, fully lit, with a computer on the desk, already running. Sweep through the building, point the cameras at the floor.

'Why the fuck is everything on? What the fuck is this place?'

Flushing sound is from the kegs for the bar. Half a dozen of them in one room, still plugged in, ready to go.

Find the trapdoor, lock it with a bolt from inside. Find the kitchen, fully equipped with freezers, fridges, microwaves, cupboards full of food. Up the stairs, find the Sitex door, shove metal into the locks. Upwards we go, find four floors of rooms, each with a dozen bunk beds crammed in at crazy angles. The water is on. The showers work.

Every room is strewn with debris, as if everyone had to leave in a hurry. Bags and clothes and duvets and pillows on every bed.

'We're only in one half of it. How do we get into the pub?'

We couldn't find a way through. We are in the residential half. The pub is inaccessible.

'Fuck it. Lock us in.'

A. nods, disappears out the door, locks it behind him. Hear him bend the Sitex back into position. Meanwhile, busy ourselves fitting steel bars from the door to the wall, create braces to prevent anyone else coming in that way.

Keep looking but there is no way through to the pub. Duval finds a roof access, prepares it as his favourite defence position since the Battle of Well Street. I take a call from Tasha.

'It's fucking weird. Everything is still on. There's a flatscreen telly — '

'Skybox! We have a working Skybox.'

'There's a skybox.'

'There's broadband! The broadband is on!'

'There's internet. It's like the Marie fucking Celeste. But we can't get into the pub.'

'If it's residential then you can be arrested. I'm not sure about this. Maybe we should get out and think again.'

I snap.

'But there's showers and beds and its clean and there's a kitchen full of food. I'm not leaving. Fuck it. Let them come. I'm not leaving another fucking building. This is ours now. Fuck them, fuck it. I'm going to sleep and I'm not fucking leaving? If you want the commercial side, then COME DOWN HERE AND CRACK IT YOURSELF!'

Over-reacting, but the week has been too much. This is too good to be true, I know, but it feels like going on holiday, like staying in a real hostel. Sit at the reception desk with my feet on the table, tinkering with the office computer.

Tasha can feel I am near breaking point.

'OK, ok. Just get some sleep. We'll send people over in a few hours.'

'Good. Tell them they don't need shit. Everything is here. Except beer. Bring beer.'

'And George?'

'Yeah?'

'Well done, love.'

It helps a lot. Smile, hang up. Me and Duval find the tiny room next door that might once have been an office. Skybox is on, we channel surf, mainly watching the 24-hour news. Find half a bottle of red wine, half a bottle of white. Take hot shower. High pressure power shower, built inside an old cupboard. Even shower gel, smelling like chemical limes. Spend the next hours drinking and looking through the debris of paperwork left behind. Owner had the place repossessed by the brewery, owing them tens of thousands. Obviously an unlicensed hostel. As the bottle drains our eyelids droop. We wait for the reinforcements.

The basement has no ventilation. We fill it with ganja smoke by the time the call comes. Nearly six in the morning.

The metal trapdoor at the back of the reception. Unscrew the metal bolt through the two doors, unhook the latch, shout for them to pull it up. Push with a shoulder, pop out into the street on the front of the pub to find Gunter and Ari smiling down at me, brandishing a bag of Zywiec.

'Welcome home, motherfuckers,' I smile at them.

They climb down into the Nadir.

The Nadir

'Guys! There's people outside!'

I'd been snoozing, curled up with Ari, in one of the bunk beds on the upper floors, one of the rooms without Sitex, and I realised it was the first time I had woken up to natural sunlight in over a month. We had gone to bed late, well into the morning, and now it felt like mid-afternoon. Duval had obviously been keeping an eye out.

With that rush of adrenaline that must come to all soldiers when they hear the sound of a shell exploding, I jumped up, pulling on my boots and hurtling down the stairs to the Sitex door. We could hear voices: two men, chatting amicably.

Then the sound of a key in the lock.

Sitex doors traditionally have two locks, one up and one down, which are removable from inside. Duval had put a piece of metal into the top lock, stopping the key from entering fully.

Those outside had unlocked the bottom one. The four of us lingered on the stairs, breathing silently, unsure of what to do.

'What the fuck? The key won't work in the top lock. Something's blocking it.'

They tried to pull the door. It bent open at the bottom where it was unlocked.

Duval went for it.

'Hello guys. This place has been occupied. We didn't damage anything getting in and this is a civil matter between us and the owners of the building.' He whispered over to us, 'It's the security firm.'

'What the fuck? Who is that in there? What the fuck are you doing in there? Open this door now.'

'We have legally squatted this building. This is a civil matter between us and the owners of the building. I'm not going to open this door.'

The guy outside started banging on the door.

'Seriously now.'

BANG.

'Open this fucking door now!'

BANG. BANG.

'You are starting to piss me off.'

'Listen mate there's nothing for you to do here. Your job is security and this place is secure. This is a — '

BANG. BANG. BANG.

'Seriously, you cunts come out of there now. If I have to crowbar open my own fucking door I'm gonna be seriously pissed off.'

BANG! BANG!

'Look just calm down pal — '

'OPEN THIS FUCKING DOOR!' BANG! 'OPEN THIS FUCKING DOOR NOW!'

The Sitex door shook and rattled furiously, yawning open where the bottom lock was undone. I was down on my knees holding on to the open lock by my fingertips, barely getting a purchase. I was very afraid of these guys getting through, but in a numb, distant kind of way. I wondered what they might do to us. I didn't feel in any shape for a fistfight. I looked around. There was a mallet on the floor next to me. All of this seemed so familiar. I got a terrible sense of deja vu.

'Right you cunts . . . ' we heard him mutter.

They went away. Duval suddenly had some inspiration.

'Get the rachet strap! Get the fucking rachet strap!'

Gunter ran off to find it. We heard him slamming around in the kitchen throwing tools about.

The security guys returned.

'Right. Are you going to open this fucking door or am I going to crowbar it open and rip your fucking heads off?'

'Listen mate . . . we are going to call the police. What you are doing is a criminal offence and you can be arrested and — '

The crowbar came through. They were using a jemmy and a crowbar in unison, jamming them into the gap and levering it open. It was like the claws of some horrendous monster trying to rip the door off its hinges. Duval was screaming.

'CALL THE FUCKING POLICE! SOMEONE CALL THE FUCKING POLICE NOW!'

The security guards outside went eerily quiet, working with relentless calm and precision to pry the door open. They had obviously done this before, so systematic and relentless was the work. Duval was hanging on to the top lock, me on to the bottom, pulling the door back each time they got purchase.

'HIT IT WITH THE FUCKING HAMMER!'

Ari picked up the mallet, and serenely began to hammer at the intruding metal talons each time they penetrated the door frame.

'You better not damage my fucking tools. Stop that!' came the sullen reply from outside.

The mallet clanged on the tips of the crowbar, forcing them back out. I could see the doorframe buckling and bending.

'WHERE'S THE FUCKING STRAP? CALL THE POLICE!'

Gunter burst back in with the rachet strap. I grabbed the top lock. We were all moving together now. Duval got the strap around the bottom lock and pulled it tight, both feet against the Sitex frame. I had the phone in one hand and was somehow calling 999.

'Please state the nature of the emergency.'

'We're being broken into! There's men here trying to break into our house!'

I gave them the address.

'YOU HAVE INJURED MY HAND! YOU HAVE DONE HARM TO ME! THE POLICE ARE ON THEIR WAY! YOU WILL BE ARRESTED!'

Duval worked as a street performer. He had a hell of a voice on him.

'What's the situation? What's your legal status?'

Fucking hell, I thought. We're battling armed intruders and the police want to know what legal right I have to be here. Surely they get calls from people being evicted by bailiffs and landlords all the time. This bitch is trying to figure out which side I'm on.

'We're legal guardians. The landlord wants us here. Look I've got to go they're trying again. Send help.'

I took the rachet strap from Duval as he ran up to the window to film who was trying to break in.

Ari calmly hammered away at the metal bars as they kept re-emerging, like some kind of carnival game. Gunter looked terrified.

The crowbars stopped. We pulled the door tightly shut and tied the bottom around the bannister of the stairs. We began cranking it tight with the rachet.

Duval yelled from upstairs: 'They're going around the back!'

'Gunter stay here. Start ringing people. Ring Tasha and A. Ring everybody! Fucking everybody! Ari, go to the trapdoor!'

We all raced through the warren of the building, me heading towards the backdoor. I was so relieved I barricaded the night before. I began checking the tension and strength of the braces, looking around for extra junk to wedge in there.

I could hear them peeling back the Sitex.

' . . . must be where they got it . . . '

'Look, they left their drill.'

Fuck. A. must have forgotten to pick it up.

There was the sound of a key in the lock. I braced myself against the door, ready to push back.

'They've locked it from the inside.'

'Barricade, mate. Fuck you,' I whispered to myself.

The sound stopped.

I held my breath.

Ari started shouting. They were at the trapdoor. As I raced through I heard Gunter on the phone to someone.

' . . . trying to break in. I don't know. Ja, we call police . . . '

As I got to Ari, she was hanging off the trapdoor with all her weight. The metal was clattering in the frame as the security guards stamped and bounced on it. I checked the bolts. It was secure.

It went quiet.

We waited for the next move.

'We'll be back later!' Someone shouted from outside.

I could hear Duval answering back. Some sort of exchange. We waited. All I could hear was blood rushing in my head.

'They're going guys,' shouted Duval.

I lit a cigarette. Me, Ari and Gunter stared at each other incredulously. Duval dropped back down the stairs.

'Aren't you fucking glad we brought the rachet strap now?'

*

Within the half hour, people from Squatopolis started dropping round, some decidedly disappointed that they'd missed the action. We were still cagey, unwilling to open the trapdoor, asking people to hang around outside in case they came back. The police came and went in a flash of impotent authority, telling us to ring if they came back.

After a while, people started getting bored. We started opening the trapdoor to let them in. I felt proud seeing the responses of people as they clambered down the stairs and started surveying the building. In the inimitable manner of borrowers, they began idly sifting through the detritus looking for useful bits and pieces that they good naturedly brought to show us and ask if they could have. We deferred all requests, still too wound up to start allowing people to tat the place. Some kids from Shoreditch figured out how to get beer from the overflow taps, and we started drinking to calm the nerves. The beer foamy and overheaded, but it tasted like victory.

A geekpunk from the Place turned up to inspect the internet, and reported joyously that you couldn't get much faster. People with laptops began ripping movies off the internet. They raided the freezer, snapping a padlock and uncovering a trove of cheap burger meat and buns that they subsequently began frying up. The whole place took on a feel of some itinerant hostel. The people outside reported to us in gales of laughter that a woman had turned up and stared incredulously at the exterior of the building:

'But I have a reservation here! I booked online months ago.'

'Well, you're welcome to stay, and it's all free now!' they retorted. She declined the offer.

We found parts of a PA system, a drum kit, a couple of amplifiers and a porn DVD. People put on clothes from upstairs, and Ari found two MP3 players in a bag that someone had left behind. We told and retold the story of what had happened that morning. Duval had somehow managed to film it on his phone, and he proudly showed the images of crowbars trying to rip open the door like he was a B-movie horror director. The shrieking and screaming only added to the ambience.

After a few hours playing together, people began to drift off, and others from Squatopolis set about making a living room upstairs where we could keep a look out on what was happening in the street outside. We made plans to keep people on watch, and studiously controlled the flow of people in and out of the building to prevent being caught out by a door left unlocked.

As night fell, we began to relax, calmed by beer and draw and the camaraderie of supporters. We weren't alone in this. People had shown up in solidarity and after a week of guerilla raids and abortive cracks, we had taken and held on to a place, and what a place it was. Gradually, people settled in to their laptops and burgers, or drifted back to Squatopolis to take speed and party.

I found a transistor radio, and claiming opener's rights, took the room on the top floor with the un-Sitexed window. I cleared some bunks out, and on a pair of big mattresses on the floor, lay down with the radio tuned to a pirate reggae station to stare blankly out the window into space.

How many times
You been down this road before?
Over and over and over again
Wheel keep on turning
Eternally cycling
Never beginning, it never end

As night time fell, I smoked the good green I'd been carrying for the comedown period and stared out the window as the sky fell darker and darker. I ate a couple of the chocolates we'd made with leftover greenleaf, settling into a mountain of cushions and opening the window to let the balmy March breeze blow through. Here at last, I'd found some peace. We'd won the reclaim attempt, and now, normally, we had some time to recuperate. The reggae played and I thought about the maroons in Jamaica, fleeing their masters for the hills to make their own communities, their own laws, in the jungles away from civilisation. I imagined what that life must have been like, to break your own chains and escape to a life in the woods. Living in some palm shack, listening to the sounds of the cicadas and feeling that breeze blow from across the mountains.

How many times?
So many, many times
How many times?
So many, many times

I met someone who was into pirate radio, back when I was an English teacher. We'd share a smoke break, chatting about systems and the rig culture, Aba Shanti-I and Kilimanjaro, Rodigan's reggae and the Notting Hill soundclashes.
'The only good system is a sound system', he'd laugh.

He let me bootleg discs of their sets and I'd lose myself in headphones sat at my desk in the sterile, unfriendly office I had to squeeze in, mind awhirl with crashing bass, bursts of digital noise, ullulating toasting, rebel sound. He'd told me how pirate radios get their antennaes out, people climbing up on to rooftops and dropping them down chimneys, hiding them from the authorities, even sealing them in with concrete to stop people getting them out. I'd liked the idea of an outlaw radio station, localised, locally loved, a rarity of community music in our disparate digital age. I'd wondered, when high up on a roof, how close I was to one of the transmitters that I so often listened to.

How many times
Must a cuckoo-clock sing?
Before he retire
Never to be seen again
To die in his house, alone
Alone and unmourned
Not free, not free, not free
But abhorred?

Edibles always make my mind wander, adding depth and tone to what the Germans call *kopfkini* — head cinema. I have never found a better form of entertainment. I drifted back to when I lived in Bournemouth for a summer — one of the sunniest spots in Britain. After six months eating beans on toast and scraping by on the dole, my first full-time job had been as a council worker. I had to put the deckchairs out on Boscombe beach at 8:30am everyday, then go around like a tax collector taking a pound off the grannies and junkies and topless ladies who gathered there to worship the sun. I had started smoking skunk every morning, blundering around on the beach in the sunshine barely able to speak sometimes, but always smiling and laughing and watching my skin turn a mahogany brown, my dreads growing blonder each day. Sometimes I got to ride the little toy train up and down the promenade, sitting there high as a kite, eyes hidden behind sunglasses, joking with the children and flirting with the constant stream of young ladies who seemed to find the council uniform so ridiculous but endearing on a young rasta.

That whole summer, I wore a dog-chain around one ankle, and I thought everyday about what it meant to be a slave to another man. No matter how good a job — it's one of the best I ever had — if it has a boss, it's never more than a gilded cage. On my last day of work, I stood on the end of Boscombe Pier, and watched a wall of fog roll in from the sea. In minutes, it went from blue sunshine summer to the biting chill of winter as the weatherfront rolled over us. As I shivered, I reached down, unhooked the chain, and flung it into the sea.

Switch on, tune in, drop out
Wipe your mind clean
Remote control
Switch on, tune in, drop out
Wipe your mind clean
Remote control

I was in a punk band at that time: a crew of young upstarts, all scratchy guitars, manic drums and blazing horns. We'd been some weird fusion of jazz, ska and noise, inside-out music, the drums rolling a manic melody whilst the guitars held the rhythm. Like the guys I grew up with, we were all going to get out, never sell out, never give in to the pressure of conformity, to workaday existence, to bills and bosses and all that bollocks. We'd laughed in the faces of people scrambling for 'real jobs', careers, houses, families. We drank and we drugged and we fucked and we didn't care what anyone thought — we knew it was all bullshit. Yet one by one, they started to slip into the relentless pressure of normality. First you take a job, then you get used to the money, then you get promoted, and before you know it, ten years have gone by and you're managing a team of upstart young kids who are laughing up their sleeves at what a sad old social eunuch you've become. Still, I see the photos of these people I used to know and they look happy with their wives and their babies, managing spreadsheets or whatever keeps them out of trouble and perpetuating the status quo.

Too many times
We reborn inna suffering, inna suffering yeah
Mind wipe clean by the glare of a TV screen
Can no longer define between
Jah-real and obscene
That box in the corner
False idolatry, yeah

The places I rented in Bournemouth, the dumps in London, often had no hot water in the depths of winter, had mould hanging off the ceiling, stank of stale beer and cigarette ash ground into the carpet. Every contract I'd ever signed had indentured me in servitude to pay cost after cost and keep the money in my pocket always on loan to someone else. Every flatmate, when chained together like that, had eventually become a competitor, the landlord finding ways to pit us against one another. In London I slaved at a job to make enough money for rent, travel and food, cramming on a train everyday like cattle to be farmed out to some school, remaining the equivalent of a fast-food worker in the biggest private education firm in the world. I finally snapped when they came in one day for a corporate pep-talk and said how they wanted to grow, and grow, and grow, and control everything in the English language from A to Z, from what you read, to where you stay. For me, the model was rotten. For years I'd got by on the idea that I was working with people, that I was in class helping people to communicate and mature. Together we laughed and we talked and we shared our experiences and I helped people develop themselves and their lives. Then the illusion came crashing down. These weren't people. They were 'clients'. I wasn't a teacher, or even a human being, I was 'front line customer service.' Once the glamour wore off, and the reality of how inhumane the use of money is to create a relationship between strangers, I could never go back.

So I went out to find the crazy ones, the ones burning too bright, the ones doing what they can to maintain their dignity, their freedom, their own way of life. I sat with the broken, the drug addicts and the drunks, met the quitters and the collaborators, met the organisers and the activist politicians-in-training, and everywhere I began to see how insidious the system is. How it's inside all of us, no matter how we might twist and turn to escape its grasp, that the illusion of freedom is one so perfectly projected that we cannot spot how we all have a policeman inside our head, how we all police one another, how because we're stepped on, we must step on others to feel some kind of brief power. All my bitchin' and moanin' and soliloquising about freedom and autonomy and liberty had lead me only to the fringes of such a world. A world of constant battle and struggle against external oppressors, rather than the internalised ones of the 'normal' world. Yet with some perspective, perhaps I could see myself being more normal than all my friends who took jobs and families and bought into the dream. I've travelled enough to see how many more people are close to these violent struggles, fighting police and landlords and starvation and insanity, than to the world of relative comfort and conformity.

How many times
So many, many times
How many times, yeah
Too many, many times
How many times?
So many, many times . . .

And in the end, perhaps all I learned was that when the music hits you, you feel no pain.

*

'Guys! There's some people outside!'

'You have got to be fucking kidding me . . . '

The sky outside was an insane cerulean, a single jet plane cutting a streak through it. I'd fallen asleep fully clothed, the radio still playing, and it felt like afternoon again. In fact, it felt like everything was repeating, that I was trapped in some mad feedback loop perpetually replaying until I slew the end of level boss.

Someone was banging on the door — fairly politely — as I staggered down the stairs towards it.

'Hello? Who's in there?'

I decided to try the classic English defence — civility.

'Hello there? How my I help you this fine morning?'

'Hello. We're from the landlord. Look, we've just come around to pick up a few things. So, if you could just open the door, we'll pop in and get them and be on our way.'

'Look we're not opening this door mate, so just give it up.'

'Listen, we want the karaoke machine and the pool table, so if you open up, we'll bung you a bit of cash and everyone's happy.'

'Look mate, there's no karaoke machine and no pool table here.'

'No they're definitely there. They're in the bar area. We'll be in and out. No problem.'

'Er . . . wait. I'll look around for them, hang on.'

'Look, I'll just go get the van, I'll be back in five minutes, ok?'

I was confused. Politeness can be confusing. It's so much more straightforward to be rude. I heard them talking to each other.

'I think these are Oliver's boys. They got in so we can get this stuff out . . . '

Duval was there, yawning and stretching. Other faces started popping out.

'There's no karaoke machine here, right?' I asked, still perplexed.

We wandered around for a bit, idly looking. None of us really knew what was going on. I checked the rachet strap and the block on the lock. No way were they getting in through there.

Ari and Gunter were making toast, and the kettle was on. We talked about the visit in a kind of distracted way, as if we were all shellshocked soldiers talking about the latest enemy incursion.

After about twenty minutes, Tasha called to be asked to be let in through the trapdoor. Someone went off and collected her. It was her first time over, and she was delighted and amazed by the relative luxury of it all. We made her some tea, thanking her profusely for the milk, and sat around in the lookout-cum-lounge we'd cleared at the top of the house.

'Well, this is a lovely little holiday home, isn't it?' said Tasha, clinking tea mugs with us.

'Oh yes, and in very high demand. You know we just had our second visit of today? This time from some people who know Oliver . . . I guess that must be the landlord. They seem to think he's hired us to open this place and get his stuff back. They offered some money.'

'Oh, really? How interesting. Still, after yesterday I really don't think we should let anyone in.'

'True. What they want is on the other side anyway. So if they want it, let them crack it and take it themselves. We're not mercenaries!'

We cackled away, so fucking delighted with ourselves.

Then there was a bang on the door.

I put down my tea and banged down the stairs.

'Hello?'

'Hello mate, it's me. We've come to pick up that stuff. Can you open up?'

'Er, listen pal, it's not here. There's no karaoke machine and no pool table. They must be next door.'

'Well, we'll come in and have a look.'

'Look, it's not here and you're not coming in. They might be next door, but there's no access from this side.'

'Look, just open the door and we'll go through and get them.'

'There's no access from this side.'

BANG! BANG!

'Just open the fucking door! Open this fucking door!'

This time, I wasn't even bothered.

'Listen mate! You want your shit — it's next door! Go crack the fucking building and get it yourself because it's not on this side!'

More banging. I almost laughed when they tried to pull

the door. The rachet strap didn't even flinch. I waited as they screamed and banged.

'LISTEN! OPEN THIS DOOR OR I'LL BE BACK HERE WITH FIFTEEN GEEZERS AND WE'LL RIP THE DOOR OFF!'

'YOU WOULDN'T BE THE FIRST ONE TO TRY PAL!'

That had come out more angrily than I had expected. Duval, Ari, Tasha and Gunter were all around, looking, waiting.

The guy disappeared.

'Fuck him,' I said.

Suddenly I heard the trapdoor go. It clattered much more loudly than it should.

Ari was there first, seeing a pair of fingers reaching in trying to undo the bolt. Someone had left it partly unlocked when they let Tasha in and now it was nearly open. Ari leapt up, grabbed the trap and yanked it down. A man yelped as his fingers were nipped. An angry booted foot stomped on the trap door. Gunter was wrapping rope around the handles, ready to pull it shut. Suddenly everyone was shouting.

' . . . call the fucking police!'

' . . . back with fifteen guys we'll fucking kill you . . . '

' . . . want to fucking try mate? I barricade all day! You come in here I eat your fucking eyes . . . '

' . . . get more rope . . . '

' . . . I do this for a living pal! Fucking come on in!'

' . . . pool table . . . '

I called the police, finger in one ear against all the hubbub. The guys outside continued stamping on the trapdoor.

'Can you please state the nature of the emergency?'

Round and round we went . . . At this point that my nerves finally went. I was the one shrieking violent threats at the people outside. They gave up shortly, muttering about being back. The police came back and did nothing. After that, I packed up my stuff and said goodbye to the Nadir, heading back to Squatopolis, where at least the raids were still scheduled. The Nadir remained a little squat holiday home, but we went through the usual motions. Papers arrived on Monday, court on Thursday, IPO served same afternoon.

Everyone cleared out by Friday.

Squatopolis Now

. . . a place in Shoreditch, where children were born and reared in circumstances which gave them no reasonable chance of living decent lives: where they were born foredamned to a criminal or semi-criminal career.

The narrow street was all the blacker for the lurid sky; for there was a fire in a farther part of Shoreditch, and the welkin was an infernal coppery glare. Below, the hot, heavy air lay, a rank oppression, on the contorted forms of those who made for sleep on the pavement: and in it, and through it all, there rose from the foul earth and the grimed walls a close, mingled stink — the odour of the Jago.

— Arthur Morrison, *A Child of the Jago*

'This is really shit.'

I awoke in the night to the piercing klaxons of a malfunctioning alarm and splashed out into a corridor boobytrapped with dogshit. The wettest winter in 250 years. Water pissing down through the concrete and bitumen, half caught in buckets with holes in the bottom, floods of rain pooling scant inches from the illegally re-rigged electricity. Squatopolis, in the heart of the East End, had come as a great relief after two weeks of barricades and cracking, but the Monday malaise and the arrival of papers quickly extinguished any previous passions for fixing up our new home.

Already tedious bickering about the washing up had returned, complaints about skipping, and yet the manor around us was crumbling and in urgent need of maintenance, love and attention. You can only swab the decks solo so many times before you start to look around at the crew and wish there was a captain flogging some of these punks. Swerving violently between hungover hunger and drunken vitriol, I was unsteady and in need of some serious R and R.

From a mighty twenty-seven people, we had shattered and split over the last two weeks, losing people to the general attrition, fatigue and travels. More than half had gone to the reopened Camden squat, the one now daubed with 'Get Rich Or Try Sharing', and had converted it into an apparently cosy faux-yuppie apartment in the heart of North London.

We, on the other hand, were roughing it in Shoreditch, another prime location, just off Brick Lane. But on that rainy Monday in April it felt, yet again, like we'd barricaded ourselves into a tomb for no good reason. Already we were counting down under our breath for when we would be booted out, hopefully to digs in better condition, and with more time to build.

The first week had been a flurry of joyous activity: we constructed a shanty town of wooden rooms, occupying two units of the monolithic warehouse with the tattered remains of the crew. It was like being shipwrecked. We vanned our possessions over, including the pathetic booty looted from the Battle of Well Street, and moved in as best we could.

After two weeks on the fly, the relief of unpacking my meagre belongings into the little wooden room with a mezzanine was palpable. I fixed a tatted spotlight, bagged a heater, and eventually we wheeled three mattresses back from the Commercial Road to complete the comforts of home. Under the moody lighting, it didn't look half so dingy, and the flooding was mildly abated by the carpets on the floor.

The dogfights and the constant drunken swagger of any and every visitor passing through quickly grew tiresome. The problem of making any previously abandoned space comfortable and liveable is that every fucker feels at home in it. Already we'd had to nip a Sunday afterparty in the bud, screaming at the random gutterpunks who'd squatted our custom-built kitchen table to take their beers and fuck off. Every morning I woke up and wanted to start drinking until I felt normal again. Running off sugar and fried fish, in a building where it rained indoors, staring at bare cupboards and empty pockets, we had smashed through the triumphalism of resistance into the grimy inaction of occupying.

*

The arrival of court papers. We know that in a week we will be judged in court and found lacking any real claim to this building, and the process will begin anew. The doorbell still jangles incessantly with people coming and going. We have lost count of how many lost souls are secreted in the strange crevasses and lacunae of this cavernous hulk. Squatopolis. We dream of the biggest squat in London, an occupied city, right of the heart of the Old East End. Instead, we sit on skipped Chesterfield sofas, smoking dogends and pilfering alcohol from each other.

The weekend began with the arrival of Possession Order papers. At least it wasn't an IPO; that would have meant bailiffs within two to three days. Now, ten days seemed like an eternity. In our usual fashion, we decided to tear out into Dalston and the boroughs around and get competently fucked up. It ended with being banned from Passing Clouds. We'd become the scum of society, the lowest dregs of amoral, feckless street trash. And I didn't care. I long ago lost any respect for the strivers, the workers, the compromisers. If you worked for money, for someone else, I saw you as a chattel, a lackey, a slave. Instead, I'd sit with no money in my pocket, waiting for the skipping hour with wet boots and an empty stomach.

I wanted to believe that this would be where it would end for me. Starving, bitter, alienated by the people both outside and within, no feeling of camaraderie, of rebellion, even of indignation any more. Just sitting around waiting for the internet to start working, the rain to stop, the skip to arrive. Just surviving. Just eking out a mangy existence on the fringe. The ideals and aspirations, the rage and passion, all seemed very far away, like strange teenage fantasies, the idealistic fluff of deluded wannabes.

Even writing this shit. Who cares about the homeless? The squatters? The radicals and addicts? Bums. Parasites. Loafers. How many times have I had 'get a job' screamed at me by strangers. 'Pay your rent.' 'Be normal.' I don't expect any different in responses to this book. Already I anticipated a sound critical panning, a muted half fart of success and then what? What the hell do I have to write about after this? No doubt the hardcore element of the squat scene will ostracise me for breaking omerta, and the lunatic fringe will be unaffected.

In the end, is this just poverty porn for *Guardian* readers, the yoghurt weavers and the comfortably revolutionary part-timers? The only thing I hope to achieve by writing these chapters is a sense of validation in a world that has labelled me scumbag, sampah masyarakat, scrounger, jago. To know that at least one person was paying attention. It is important to record these moments, these slices of reality, whether victorious or despondent, without descending into shoe gazing or self-congratulation.

*

'We fit into the spaces in between,' said Osmond, sat on the concrete floor of a cavernous factory unit at 5am, brandishing a black banana at me and babbling. The meth had got him. Weeks of speed and an opportune run-in with a fellow crystal conspirator meant that he had succumbed to his old vice. I doubted he'd slept in a week. His sparkling blue eyes were manic, sunken into a hollow face half hidden in a feral beard. He had been wandering around all night hallucinating about a family living on the roof. Paranoia held him tight to its chest. Staying in a mouldy room, within days he would have a lung infection and force himself to move out to a sober, stable squat where he could put himself back together.

I vowed I'd never take meth again.

I learn to grab those moments, between mind numbing exhaustion and speed-freak intensity. To savour an evening of film blasted through a street speaker in womb-like warmth. Learn to love the peace and tranquillity, not to lapse into total lethargy and apathetic malaise. Live my life, between the barricades and the police raids, between the strikes of bailiffs and the outbreaks of manic collective psychosis.

'I didn't go to work today . . . '
' . . . and I don't think I'll go tomorrow.'
The braying laughter follows.
'No work today.'

Take the time to cook meat skipped off the street with soggy bananas and a cache of spices, shared over a miniature bottle of wine and tall tales of the crazies and reprobates we'd kicked out of our doors. Leaf through the abandoned tomes and scrolls left behind in crumbling textile warehouses, gleaning scraps of knowledge and interpretation of radical history, anthropology and the humanities. Compose lists of anarchist assassins and bankrobbers from yesteryear, those who threw bombs and shot kings.

Ari came back into the den where I was conscientiously rejecting consciousness, wallowing in my sleeping bag on a stale pillow and insisting to the world, 'not just yet'.

'I'm not comfortable opening the door. It's the kids from Whitechapel.'

Grumbling, craving tea and nicotine, I pulled on my sweat shorts and flopped down to the heavy iron gate in my laceless boots. Someone was rolling down to let themselves out, and as we grated the door aside, the Whitechapel kids greeted me with raised cans of Polish lager and a barrage of requests. I blocked them in the door, one girl physically stepping back as she felt my unwelcoming vibe.

'We just come round to take a shower and hangout.'

It was the loud Irishman we'd booted out of our kitchen not two days prior. The others were vaguely familiar.

'How many of you want a shower?'

'Just me.'

'I'm not dealing with it guys. There's nobody here you know and I'm not babysitting you guys.'

A howl of derision and disgust. People like us always hate not to get what they want.

'Look, you're all pissed and I just woke up. You can't come in.'

'Oh well, we were gonna give you a beer but if you're going to be like that then you get nothing!'

As they dangled the beers in front of me, I felt my resolve weakening.

'Just fuck off.'

'Yeah well, anything you ever need mate, don't hesitate to ask, yeah?'

The sarcasm was dripping. I slammed the door shut in their faces.

I wasn't even halfway back to the Unit when the doorbell went again. I turned about-face and marched right back, picking up a lump of 2 x 4 as I went like it was the most normal thing in the world to answer a door with.

'Hello?'

It was two more Whitechapel guys, but these two I did know, one of them well enough that I was happy to let them in, even though he was clutching a bottle of lifted red wine. As I did, the lad who wanted a shower bundled in as well. His face was an angry mask. He was sat at the kitchen table by the time I got back, and I walked in on him audibly complaining about me.

'Listen man, you're in now, just go and have your shower. Don't sit around here getting pissed.'

'I'm not even drunk mate I just had one can.'

'Look man just see it from the otherside. We had trouble with that Irish guy here before, it's early, I just woke up, my girl dumped this problem on me. What would you do?'

'Yeah, well, solidarity mate.'

My heart sank. Chinning his can of beer he sent it clanging it into the recycling. He sloped off to the shower.

Left behind in the Unit kitchen, I found the wine drinkers.

'I understand why you did that. That's what we should have done at Whitechapel all along. You heard about what happened last night? Absolute carnage. We had to kick out four people last week. Long stay guests. But that guy is alright. He would do anything for you, for anyone. He's solid.'

I was troubled, cursing as I drank more tea. I hated the idea that a complete stranger would have that image of me, but I wasn't going to stretch to let in these people I didn't know. They would be my responsibility if I let them through the door.

I went out into the corridor and found the shower kid.

'Mate. I want to apologise. I don't want to make you feel shit first thing in the morning. It's nothing personal against you. We just have to take responsibility for who we let in. When you said solidarity, it broke my heart. I don't want to be a dick. We just have to protect ourselves and our space.'

He smiled. He was young, maybe a decade younger than me. He whipped out a hand and we shook. Now we were connected better, a deeper understanding, an individual pulled from the faceless mob. When I let him out later, he looked at me again and said with a smile: 'I know you from somewhere mate.'

We fist-bumped, easy and natural, and I felt redeemed. Living like this, reputation becomes all-important, and you can make enemies easily in a world where grudges stick. At least now I felt like I had an ambassador to go back to speak to the others about what had happened on the door that morning.

*

'You know I have made hundreds of people homeless.'

I hadn't seen Judge Stone in years, not since the ramshackle rabble of the King's Court trouped into Number 10 Gee Street years before. I wondered idly whether Rudyard was still alive. Stone looked greyer, morose, and perhaps due to the much smaller crowd this time, more softly spoken.

He gave the same pronouncement as years before, agreeing to allow the defence to speak if they be tied by name to the costs. The claimant's lawyer was slick, young but earnest. The usher introduced us, and I confessed immediately that we intended to enter no defence against their claim, instead angling to negotiate for more time to vacate. The desperation with which I pitched to her was only half a performance, fuelled by borderline mania after three days of sleepless cruising debauchery, staggering around an abandoned warehouse complex.

I'd seen Stone apoplectically dissect a poorly written defence, and his pedantic yet remorseless commitment to the letter of the law. He wanted to know if there was a risk of 'exceptional hardship' if he did not immediately grant possession. I thought about the guy we lived with one lung, who had been heaving in his room the morning we staggered to court. When I told Stone, he dismissed it, as he wasn't here. I told him he was too ill to come, having the one lung and all.

*

I need to get out of here. I can't sleep properly, I'm doped and drunk half often as not. How long can this go on? I have become the dregs, the leftovers, the loud drunk and the manic druggy, the one that fell off the bottom rung and into the gutter overflowing with scum. No pretensions left, other than total rejection of society. Now I don't even blink as I pick a dog end up off a busy City street; flip the lid of a container bin and lean deep inside; turn up hammered on homebrew and aguardiente at the housewarming party and slur incoherent slogans whilst badly playing a guitar with three strings. Yet I still can't ignore the doorbell and walk through three rooms and a hundred-metre corridor, past dozens of people perfectly capable of opening the door, to let in someone I don't even know.

*

We climbed in over the gate to get a better look at the rambling mezzanines and hallways leading between each of the units. We waited until the guard in the last section went home for the night, and the builders over the road eyed us suspiciously as we loitered around the alleyways behind Great Eastern Street.

On the roof, we sat under a fire escape to smoke a cigarette and ponder the access routes we'd discovered. Across from us, the Hoxton Hotel loomed like a derelict ocean liner. Only one window was illuminated, a single square of light burning in the uppermost floor. The speed freak I was with nudged me.

'Can you see what I can see?'

I looked, and looked again. Framed perfectly in the window was a young woman in black frilly lingerie, her makeup and hair done in a 1920s flapper style. She wiggled her hourglass hips, snapping the tops of her stockings and then coquettishly grabbed her boobs and waggled them in the boned corset. The speed freak and I watched mesmerised, checking our position to confirm that we were nigh on invisible, hidden in the shadows beneath the stairwell. We hissed to our comrade who was stomping about in the moonlight.

As he ducked in beside us, the girl disappeared, and a topless man replaced her. He was talking animatedly. We saw him bend over and make the inimitable motion of snorting a line off the table in front of the window. Then he too vanished.

Dumbstruck at the little intimate vignette we'd witnessed, we lingered on the roof for a few moments more, awaiting the next installment of this Shoreditch soap opera. Then a grimy feeling descended upon us. We were here to scout a home, not to voyeur on hipsters living it up at the Hoxton. The seedy stickiness of it all was too much, and we slunk back down the building and off back to Squatopolis, escaping from the vision of a world somehow familiar yet totally alienating.

The building behind the Hoxton Hotel was cracked two days later. The guys who took it saw another squatter crowbar the door off a neighbouring unit like a breaking ninja, a swing of the shoulders before disappearing inside. By the afternoon, the security guards returned with paperwork proving the section they occupied was listed as residential, the council tax forms proving the illegality of their occupation, and they were back in Squatopolis within 24-hours of opening.

We need a win. We need a safe place. Everyone is holding their breath.

The next day, we find it.

The location is perfect. A yard, overgrown with trees, right by the railway arches, just the highest windows peeking over their tops, not even visible from the street.

'I got lost yesterday evening and found it. A fox ran under the gate and I followed him through.'

'It's perfect. A real find.'

We need to get lucky and soon. People are unravelling in every direction. We are out on a limb after enjoying the comforts of Camden and the community there. After Hackney and here, I realised that the bonds are spread too thin.

I hide here from the world. And it's wonderful. The numbness I felt in my other lives, the routine and the regularity, is torn violently away each day and cast aside. Daily I'm stripped, flogged, ignored, judged. And it doesn't matter, because I do so much that they do not. Stone was doing the same things five years ago, speaking from the same script. Inbetween so much has happened that it would be incomprehensible to this man who had never been homeless. Routine had saved his life.

It could all go wrong so fast. Whenever I was here, it seemed to.

*

The arguments of drunken lovers brokering open relationships pierce through the booming sound system playing in an empty room next door. The threat of installing a pissjug in protest at a part of the communal room becoming an ad hoc dog toilet. The pack of stoners who seem to have disappeared after consuming the joint of anonymous meat that had been festering on the kitchen table for three weeks. Me and Ari tearing emotional holes in each other, fighting and fucking and drinking and loving and hating, our screams of sexual ecstasy and immutable despair interchangeable and often indecipherable. This was what we were fighting for.

It's called exposure. People without shelter start to suffer from it after too much prolonged discomfort in the outdoors. It becomes hard to concentrate, to follow a narrative, a development. You end up stuck in the present tense. Surviving. Grasping at each moment looking for peace, shelter, calm. All the insanity out there, the heaving streets of London, the chaotic and twisted guts of this building, all squirmy with human parasites, wriggling in a concrete intestine of Shoreditch. At least here in my den, with my half-shut door and my possessions of hand-me-down, street-found tat, I can savour a moment of tranquillity. The hum of a fan heater intermingles with the rolling sonorous wave of cargo-trains passing by. Occasionally the mice nesting in the wall next to my pillow rearrange their furniture fustily. At any moment, the peace could be shattered.

It was shattered by laughter.

For that's the other side, always possible, that the atmosphere can change, as everything can change, and will. The joy of one moment, the bitterness of the next. Creation and destruction, ebb and flow, are forces always close by, like waves on a beachhead. It really depends on how much responsibility you take. Life is part what happens to you, part what you make happen. Where shall we live? How shall we live? With the larger constraints removed we can experiment with autonomy in such questions. I am responsible, solely, rather than as a boss or employee.

Decide your own level of involvement.

*

With both arms and a foot braced against the wall, I slid the massive iron door open and let the spring air blow off Brick Lane into the fetid bowels of Squatopolis. The Editor stood there in the sunshine, smiling amiably.

'Morning.'

'Morning mate. How's it going?'

'Yeah we had quite the morning of it. A. went out at six am on his bike and spotted the bailiffs assembling just round the corner. He came back and woke everyone up and we were in position before they even got here.'

I slammed the metal door shut, shoving the piece of twisted metal that served as a lock back into the hole.

'We had people up on the roof scouting for them. Maybe ten bailiffs with twenty odd coppers in support. Dog units. The whole shebang. They spent twenty minutes cutting the padlocks off that door before they realised we had welded it shut. Denied.'

'Crikey.'

We moved down the long front corridor that connected all the different units. At the second door a barricade stretched from the wooden frames all the way back to the wall. We climbed through it like children through an adventure playground.

'Next they came at this one with the angle grinders. The whole place filled with smoke as they tried to cut in. The noise, man, you can't imagine the noise. It was like Hell was breaking in. My mate filmed what was happening outside. One of the girls charged at the cutter and threw a bottle of water at it. The copper shoved her and she went skidding across the road on her arse. Easily five metres. Ballsy, mate, very ballsy. Cup of tea?'

'Oh lovely. Cheers.'

We went through to Unit 4 where we'd managed to build a reasonable fascimile of a kitchen in the hollow cavern of the former textile house.

'Next they tried to crowbar this window here. They were cutting through it when my mate stuck his arm out and held on to it. It was at that point that the police called it off. Sugar?'

'Two please.'

'Of course we had a little party to celebrate and most people are sleeping it off now, but I managed to stay awake to see you. Line of speed?'

'Er . . . I'm alright thanks.'

'Yeah I mean this is the second time. County court last week, high court one week later. It's unheard of. They really want us out of this shithole. Last week they made us take down the banner that says, 'Nazis fuck off.' We asked them why and they said, 'because it'd offend people'. We laughed in their faces and said, "Only fascists like you." Ha ha.'

'Wow.'

'Well, it's business as usual. We got a call at 8am the other day from a squatted pub round the corner and got over in time to watch the cops seal the street, don riot gear, and smash their way through the door whilst the bailiffs laughed and some dodgy geezers in tracksuits wandered around cackling. Totally illegal. Two punks arrested inside. Madness. They literally don't give a fuck, the fucking fuckers. Still, at least for the weekend we get to stay here. Today we won. Today we did OK.'

'Nice one.'

'Come on, grab your tea and I'll give you a tour. There's a full size skatebowl on the second floor that the local graffers came round and decorated the other day . . . '

Acknowledgements

The author would like to thank first of all his editor Gary, and Kit from Influx Press, for their hard work and dedication, without which this book would never have been finished.

Thanks also to the White Rhino crew for kickstarting the adventure, to the Krü Kru crew for taking me in when my life fell apart and making me part of their family; to the Bonobo crew for showing me what could be done with an empty furniture shop; and to all the other squatters and radicals who touched my life during these past years.

Also thanks to my brother B. for the three hour debate on squatting at his stag do; and to my parents for leaving me to make my own choices and mistakes.

Much love and thanks to all the people of the Welcome Community Home in Malaysia, and the members of the Fallen Leaves Theatre for helping me learn about horizontalism and the power of performance.

Thanks to the photographers who allowed their work to be reproduced here.

Above all, thanks, love and liberty to the many, many people who have struggled in solidarity to shelter themselves and others in the midst of massive global wealth disparity and housing catastrophe.

ACAB/ABAB

Whatever they say, squatting will stay.

Further Reading

Hakim Bey — *T.A.Z: The Temporary Autonomous Zone* (1985)

Augusto Boal — *Theatre of the Oppressed* (1979)

Alfredo M.Bonanno — *Armed Joy* (1977)

Noam Chomsky — *Imperial Ambitions: Conversations on the Post 9/11 World* (2005)

Mark Fisher — *Capitalist Realism* (2009)

Mansuoba Fukuoka — *The One Straw Revolution* (1975)

Peter Gelderloos — *To Get to the Other Side* (2010)
Anarchy Works (2010)
How Nonviolence Protects the State (2005)

Bolton Hall — *Three Acres and Liberty* (1918)

Stewart Home — *Down and Out in Shoreditch and Hoxton* (2004)

Peter Kropotkin — *Fields, Factories and Workshops* (1912)

Wolfi Landstreicher — *Against the Logic of Submission* (2005)

Errico Malatesta — *Anarchy* (1891)

Antonio Negri / Michael Hardt — *Multitude* (2004)

George Orwell — *Down and Out in Paris and London* (1933)

Hans Prujit — *The Logic of Urban Squatting* (2013)

Henry David Thoreau — *Walden* (1874)

Colin Ward — *Cotters and Squatters* (2004)
              Anarchy in Action (1973)

Howard Zinn — *A People's History of the United States* (1980)

About the Author

George F. is a writer, performance poet and natural farmer who has travelled extensively across Europe and Asia working with socially excluded groups ranging from the homeless in London to heroin addicts and street kids in Kuala Lumpur.

Total Shambles is his first book.

You can read more of his articles and interviews at: www.thelifeanarchic.com.

INFLUX
PRESS

Influx Press is an independent publisher specialising in writing about place.

We publish challenging, controversial and alternative work written in order to dissect and analyse our immediate surroundings, to blur genres and to produce site-specific fiction, poetry and creative non-fiction.

www.influxpress.com

A BAN treating all squatters as criminals regardless of circumstances is a nonsense. Near where I live this summer a squat called Well-Furnished was established in properties that had been empty up to four years. Before it arrived, the trust that owns most of the property locally had hiked rents and shops had closed. The squat welcomed locals to do crafts or develop their trade in the space and classes were offered in everything from Spanish to crocheting. The squatters approached the trust repeatedly to negotiate a deal to stay for a fixed time and upgrade the building but they were just turfed out at 6am one day. Leaving property empty for years is a bigger social problem than squatting – do we want inner London to be like central Paris, where only the rich can live?

Praise for *Total Shambles*

Total Shambles is a fantastic piece of work, everything that writing should be — funny, moving, exciting, wild. A history lesson, a polemic, a picaresque adventure story, and, at big and pulsing heart, an attack on the shameless, state-encouraged worship of money and power and possessions and the tiny-mindedness and shrivelling of soul that is its consequence. Proof, if any more were needed, of the necessity of disobedience. It also contains the best description of a ketamine hit I've ever read.

— Niall Griffiths, author of *Grits*, *Sheepshagger* and *Runt*

Dodgy on the edge, or edgy on the dodge? Either way, George F.'s thunderous declamation against the enforced poverty of those who choose to exist on the other side of the lines, and possibly beyond the pale, acts as a salutary lesson in the florid hardships and plain hard work of 'alternative lifestyles': you can make it if you can take it. Few can.

— Penny Rimbaud, Crass

Life behind the Sitex door. The highs and lows of late London squatters, from eviction to addiction. Glimpses of community among the homeless, direct from the anarcho-underbelly of the London property boom. A series of confrontations from the contested margins of urban living, full of stories about how to live when there is (apparently) nowhere to live.

— Professor George McKay, author of *Senseless Acts of Beauty: Cultures of Resistance since the Sixties*, *DiY Culture* and *Radical Gardening*